Dr. A.P.J. Abdul KALAM
Biography of A Saintly Scientist

Dr. A.P.J. Abdul Kalam

Biography of A Saintly Scientist

A.K. Gandhi

Ocean Books Pvt. Ltd.
ISO 9001:2015 Publishers

No part of this publication can be reproduced, stored in a retrieval system or transmitted in any form or by any means, electronic, mechanical, photocopying, recording or otherwise without the prior permission of the author and the publisher.

Published by
Ocean Books (P) Ltd.
4/19 Asaf Ali Road,
New Delhi-110 002 (INDIA)
e-mail: info@oceanbooks.in

ISBN 978-81-8430-495-4
Dr. A.P.J. Abdul Kalam
Biography of A Saintly Scientist
by Shri A.K. Gandhi

Edition
2021

Price
₹ 400.00 (Rupees Four Hundred only)

© Reserved

Printed at
Narula Printers, Delhi

Author's Note

Dr. Kalam had many shades to his personality. He started his working life as an engineer and scientist, and in this capacity, undertook several projects of national importance and helped to make the country self-dependent in those domains. As a Scientific Advisor and Principal Scientific Advisor, he expanded his horizons and worked well beyond the realms of science with a view to bring solace and empowerment to the suffering masses. He worked on his visions of India 2020 and PURA; and these remain the goals of the succeeding governments. As the President, he laid down several norms which would be difficult for the successors to flout. And then as a teacher and inspirational speaker, he did the most important job, that was to motivate the young people and helped them tide over their negative feelings. People called him the Missile Man, People's President and Interactive President, but if you asked me, I would say that he was a true Social Worker. Had he wanted, he could have rested his limbs to enjoy the fruits of his work at any stage of life; but no...he did not rest until his very last moment; when he breathed his last, he was doing what he loved best...to speak to the young people at the IIM, Shillong.

Being in his company is a moment of joy, as anyone blessed with this opportunity will concur. Dr. Kalam respected every person...he looked at every being as a personality...a unique personality. For him, being up or down the hierarchical order in a department or society was just an arrangement by which it could function well. He attached as much importance to the highest functionary as he attached to the lowest person in a hierarchy. He said that there could not be a leader without a follower, there could not be an officer without a peon, and there could not be a queen without a maid. These are the titbits of jobs that combine together to take a giant shape. If you came to call on him, he would walk to the door to see you off, irrespective of the rank or status of the visitor, so humble he was.

Dr. Kalam was a learner all his life. He commanded subjects beyond his realm of work. He felt home with science as well as social subjects, he did not allow anything to escape his notice, and he wanted to know everything. As he toured different parts of the country and world, he made bid to learn, and whenever he had a doubt, he would consult books and people to overcome it. He was a widely read man, and turned out to be a writer with several books to his credit. You can find a subtle transformation in his language when he deals with different subjects. His favourite topics were science, development, spirituality and social causes; and he could sail from one topic to another with spontaneous ease.

Dr. Kalam was born and brought up in a multi-religious, multi-ethnic community, and this type of milieu had a profound effect on his personality. He gave equal respect to all faiths and religions; and he did not pay only lip-service to different religions. During his life, he visited the saints and seers of all faiths, discussed with them and learnt from them. He learnt what divinity and spirituality actually meant, and brought out a blended form. For him, religion is a connecting thread. He was quite at ease when he quoted from the Gita or the Hadith, or for that matter, from the holy texts of other faiths.

In this book, we have made a solemn endeavour to read his mind, how he thought at every turn of his life; and this will help the readers to understand the intricacies of his thinking and how he was guided for a mission in his life. To understand him well, we have also narrated a number of incidents, accidents and events of his life, that would contribute to holistic understanding about him. He took up the challenges and worked on them wholeheartedly; whenever he failed, he overcame his negativity and came out a stronger man than ever. This is the beauty of his character, and this makes him one of the most popular public figures of all times.

May his soul rest in peace!

—**A. K. Gandhi**

Contents

Author's Note	5
1. Indomitable Spirit	11
2. Early Life	15
3. The First Step	29
4. Failure is a Stepping Stone	36
5. Working Life	40
6. The First Leap	48
7. The Missile Man	68
8. The Next Phase	98
9. Retirement is Still Away	109
10. Ascent to the Rashtrapati Bhavan	113
11. As President of India	117
12. The Job that Kalam Loved Best	148
13. Influences	152
14. Resolving Entanglements	157
15. Vision	163
16. Abiding Values	173
17. Inspiring Stories from Life of Dr. Kalam	182
Bibliography	197

1

Indomitable Spirit

The Tricolour was flying gloriously atop the school building overlooking the expansive lawns in which, on either side of the narrow road leading to the main gate, we had lined up. The principal was kind enough to allow me to stand with the teachers, and I looked just one of them, holding a bowl of petals in my hand, off and on looking to the road; obviously we were waiting for a special personality, who had taken the hearts of all people by storm. We were waiting for none else but Dr. A.P.J. Abdul Kalam.

Whenever I got a chance to see him, I thought it a special day for me; anyway, he was the supreme commander of the armed forces, of which I had been a part: a soldier is a soldier all his life, even after retirement. The sight of the supreme commander fills a soldier's heart with hope and optimism; and this was one of the two reasons I had to convince the principal for permission to be there. For this occasion, I had decorated on my chest my medals which I had received during my service with the Indian Air Force. I had more affinity with him. In fact, people from all over India wrote him letters; and they wrote in their own languages. Whenever he received a letter or presentation in Hindi, it came to me for translation; and I enjoyed every one of it. In the beginning, I had taken Dr. Kalam to be one of the VIPs, but through the letters, I could see his earnestness and sincerity to his mission; he read even the acknowledgements sent to him. He wrote comments in his own hand. As I thought all about this, the silence was only disturbed by the peals of laughter that often issued from the students lining next to us, who adorned silence once again only when the teachers looked at them with stern eyes.

All this did not go on for long when a shining car stopped before the gate, and from it emerged the person we were so curiously waiting for. As soon as he saw the children lining before him, a broad smile spread on his lips, but he wanted to take a stock of the entire scenario first, so he looked up, and found the Tricolour flying in all glory. His right hand went up to his forehead and then he once again looked towards the children. I could not understand whether he was saluting the Tricolour or the children; both of whom resided in his heart equally well.

The principal welcomed Dr. Kalam and as he walked past me amidst the flower shower, I saluted in the perfect Air Force style, and he glanced at me, perhaps recognising the soldier in me, which was quite manifest from the medals shining on my chest, giving a small jerk to his face. My heartbeat hard at this kind gesture. Smiling and waving his hand to students gently, he disappeared in the school building while the teachers guided students to the auditorium.

I simply cannot forget the occasions I found this great personality in my proximity; he inspired even without saying a word, and when he spoke, he mesmerised the listeners with his straightforward and honest views. Whoever came into his contact once wanted to be with him on more occasions; perhaps this was the reason that I liked to be at the place near my hometown where he was scheduled to visit.

Unfortunately, his death has created a vacuum that cannot be filled. He was a People's President in true sense of the word. In the coming pages, we shall try to explore the shades of his personality at different turns of his life to find out how he attained this magnificent epithet.

Dr. Kalam wanted to be in the company of children and young people because he seemed to nurture a vision in them. He wanted all aspects of life to embrace science, but he knew that science has also been the cause of conflict…and there have been numerous occasions when there have been conflicts between people, between races, between nations and between alliances…they are eternal, and several go on today. In the light of science, he did not want to lose sight of the fact that science can also prove to be a destructive force for the mankind, and he did not want the world to end on a sordid note; he wanted life to thrive in an ever better manner; and he had found this idea contained in the Islamic doctrine of *me'rafat*. This term, according to him, is a wide term and is analogous to the well-known terms *bodhi* (enlightenment or self-realisation) as per Buddhism or *mukti* (emancipation) as per Hinduism. He went among the young people to say that we should not limit our endeavours at education in a very simplistic sense, to learn some skills or to be able to earn your livelihood. He saw the role of education much beyond this limited concept; he wanted them to inculcate the spirit of good judgement and wisdom. He wanted education to create a confluence where the shades of different cultures amalgamate into a complete union, leaving their unique shades behind, to emerge into a national identity, doing good for the international community. He often called attention to countless moments in history which inflicted terrible misery and turmoil and upheaval in the world, and advised the young minds to think for a safeguard. To him, a youth with a liberal attitude and practical wisdom was the only hope, only he could provide a safeguard so that the world might be protected from any more miseries, any more turmoil and any more upheavals. This topic was near to his heart, and in his last address, at IIM, Shillong, he spoke about this; before he stopped speaking for all times to come, he was exhorting the students how to make this world a better place to live.

Though he himself was a great scientist, he did not want the children to be mere votaries of science, he wanted them to be 'thinker scientists'. Education is not something that we have devised over a few years, it comprises aspirations and ambitions of ages, learning from the instances that emerged in-between, shaping culture and civilisation, yet remaining a tool which needed to be shaped with the changing times. It is the temples of learning where the age-old wisdom is transmitted to the young minds, so it is very important that this is infused into their hearts and souls in a right set of mind. No faith or culture can survive in isolation, as no man can survive in isolation. Man is a social being, his progress can be ensured in the society; and anyone who did not need society ought to be a beast or a God: Dr. Kalam wanted children to become none of them; he wanted them to be humans, with scientific skills woven into cultural traits, with the eyes raised to the highs of progress that can be achieved during the lifetime of a man.

Dr. Kalam lived a spectacular life. He contributed to the country and world his finest; and he could have rested in the shade of his glory, enjoying the glamour that his hard work fructified into; but no, he chose to go among the young students, until the very last breath, so that his mission of life could not be lost into oblivion after he was no more. Sadly, we saw him slump on 15 October, 2015 just when he was doing what he loved to do best, speaking to the students at the IIM Shillong. He may not be there amongst us today, but his indomitable spirit continues to rule over our hearts and minds; and this book is an eulogy to this great soul.

❑

2
Early Life

Rameswaram is a place of pilgrimage where every Hindu wishes to visit at least once, and there are countless of them who visit it every year. As per the *Ramayana*, the great epic written by Valmiki, it was the place where Rama prayed to Lord Shiva to absolve him of any sins that he might have committed during the legendary battle of 'good over evil', or with Ravana, the demon king. Owing to Rama's worship here, it came to be known as Rameswaram, an epithet for Lord Shiva, literally meaning the 'Lord of Rama'. The place became prominent for the Hindus, so they visited the place in hordes.

During the middle period, this place saw the emergence of Islam, and saw several Islamic rulers, giving rise to Islam here. And, in the present times, the confluence of civilisation was as good as complete when this place came under the rule of the British in 1795, with which Christianity too made its presence felt here.

It was in this multi-cultural, multi-religious, multi-ethnic society that on 15 October, 1931, Jainulabdeen and Ashiamma were thankfully blessed with a son. The boy opened his eyes in a modest setting, not far from the Ramanathswamy Temple on Pamban Island. Right from his childhood, the child Abdul felt that everything around him was part of a greater whole. The call for prayer from the mosque, the church bells and the temple music all seemed to maintain their peculiar identity, yet they as well seemed to endeavour to blend into a wider spectrum of the whole, to help the place assume its wholesome shape. The entire scenery seemed to become brighter but sabre with the other entities in its embrace, like the sea and its rising waves, the moon and its silvery spell, the seagulls and the flutter of their wings, the sand and the transient marks being formed by the wind, the children playing on the beach and gathering shells, the pilgrims moving in search of inner peace: all this and more seemed to form part of the greater and divine arrangement of things.

Man is a mixture of heredity and environment, psychology says, Abdul Kalam, affectionately called Azad in the family, was the last of the five children of Jainulabdeen and Ashiamma, a middle-class family. The family could not boost of any great educational or financial status. His mother hailed from a prominent Tamil Muslim family. An ancestor in her family had been even bestowed the title of Rai Bahadur by the British. Not long after Azad's birth, Jainulabdeen became the Imam of the local mosque, mainly because of his impeccable character and congenial ways; he maintained absolutely harmonious relations with the religious heads of other faiths: Pakshi Lakshamana Shastrigal, the chief priest of the Rameswaram Temple; and Rev. Father Bodal, the Christian priest who also built St. Antony's Church at Oriyur.

As Azad grew up in the grand amalgamation of different faiths, mainly influenced by the presence of multitude of Hindu pilgrims, he grew to be a personality what many would like to term 'secular'. He observed how people around him stuck to their respective religions, yet bent the sacred rules to accommodate others, leading to the prevalence of a perfect harmonious culture. The child received love and affection not only at home but outside too. He learnt the way livelihood was earned in the family; how the family strove to make both ends meet; so did the people outside the home. Dignity of labour was taking shape

Early Life

within him, but he was destined for a higher realm of things, so his parents paid heed to his needs of education; more so, he was a little better than his siblings so far this aspect of life was concerned.

He received education not only at school but also at home. It came to him not in the form of letters and words, but in the form of wide experiences of life that he received at both places. The modern attitude of his parents gave him a good environment. He was sent to an Arabic school which he joined with the children of his faith; but his father wished him to have a broader spectrum of life, so he made bid to teach him other subjects, so Abdul also went to the village elementary school; it was a place where different children from different cultures and faiths intermingled under the guidance of Hindu teachers. Azad soon caught the attention of his teachers with his childlike innocence nurturing a brilliant mind and outlook. In particular, one teacher, Muthu Iyer ensured that the child cultivated a spirit in him that was destined to overcome all kinds of barriers in life; this teacher blended discipline and affection so finely that helped to shape a personality set to shine on the horizon like a splendid sun in the times to come. Naturally, the teacher became a friend of the family.

The reason why Dr. Kalam found himself quite comfortable in the company of any religious teacher and scholar can be found in his childhood. The environment in which different faiths blended was further given a boost by the friends he had. His most trusted friends came from the orthodox Brahmin families. So fast was the bond between them that he continued to recall their names and the little acts until the last; they were: Ramanadha Sastry, Aravindan and Sivaprakash. If anyone pointed out the distinction between them, Azad would wonder if they ate rice in a different way or if they loved their mother any differently.

This town continued with its age-old harmonious and coherent ways of living, while the rest of India was seeing bouts of communal tension and upheaval, which tended to grow stronger as independence came nearer. The bond between communities had been cemented with a number of incidents in which even Azad's family had contributed. In one incident, his great-great-grandfather helped to retrieve the idol of the local Ramanathaswamy Temple from the pond where it had fallen during its course of *Parikrama* (going round the town) ceremony. As the idol sank, people looked in horror if it meant death knell for them. But Azad's ancestor never thought second time before jumping into the water and emerged with the idol in his hands. Was the idol defiled? Such a narrow idea never flashed in any mind. All of them took the saviour as the hero, and as a mark of honour, he would be given Mudal Marayadai each year at the time of festival. This meant that on the occasion of festival each year, the temple would first honour him, or give Mudal Marayadai; his being from a different religion did not mean anything. This was the type of harmonious environment that prevailed in the town in which Azad was being nurtured.

His interaction with science and its capacity to build great things out of simple natural materials came early in life. He was not yet six years old when his father started a venture to build a wooden boat with the purpose to carry pilgrims to Dhanushkodi. In fact, the presence of a large number of pilgrims on the island had an economic effect on the lives of the inhabitants, and Azad's family was no exception. The child saw his father and Ahmed Jallaluddin working on the boat. Jallaluddin later married Azad's sister, Zohra. As the two men planned and seasoned the wood to shape it into a sailing boat, the child stood over them watching and trying to know what and why they were doing certain things. In this bid, he would try to help them as best as he could; of course, he could not do much at that tender age. He was fascinated when his father showed him how one plank of wood was different from the other in its density and what it meant, and what needed to be done to protect it

Early Life

from the water. In his imagination, he was beginning to notice the fine distinctions between different varieties of the same material; he now curiously touched different types of clothes to know how they were different from each other, much like the planks of wood.

When the boat was ready and took to the sea, Azad would find some opportunities on holidays to slip into the boat for a trip among the pilgrims, and it was on such occasions that he came in touch with different colours of our national culture. As his outlook widened and enriched by the experiences he received from them, he would keep asking the same questions again and again until he was satisfied. Asking questions is a great treasure for a budding scientist, and he was one. As a grown-up man, Dr. Kalam never sent back a child unsatisfied who wanted to know a thing from him. He says: "These are whats and whys that inculcate the scientific spirit in them."

Whenever the child Azad ferried in the boat, he heard what the pilgrims talked, and he often asked them his own innocent questions, which became better informed ones with time. He wondered how the monkey army built the bridge, and he often tried to find out the scientific facts about this. His scope of knowledge widened because there were pilgrims who talked about different topics; they talked about society, politics, trade and science. He was captivated by the details of each domain, and he kept inferring from the facts that came to him. He often asked the pilgrims about anything he could not understand well, and analysed it further with Jallaluddin and his father, and if his curiosity remained unfulfilled, he asked his teachers about them. And this was how the formative mind was taking a great shape. During these small voyages, his love for the sea grew too. He loved to be in the company of the lashing waves, giving out shells of a great variety, the seagulls flying over the horizon, the sun sinking behind the water, and the people climbing up the coconut trees. But what fascinated him more than anything else was the sea birds how they flew, turned, soared and dived. In fact, this interest sprang from a classroom experience. His teacher, Muthu Iyer was teaching the class about avian flight. Iyer explained to the little minds how birds take off and fly, diving and soaring in search of food and joy. Despite his best efforts, Azad was not sure if he had mastered the topic, and he said it so. Unperturbed, Iyer took the children to the seashore to show them the fine nuances how the birds flap their wings, how they move the tail, how they raise and lower the heads, and how all these activities contribute to their movements in the air. The practical lesson was far more interesting and instructive; it did a good thing to the child Azad, he learnt a lesson of the lifetime: Observe things minutely.

The innocent mind now started to look at things in more ways than one. Azad enjoyed the nature but also thought about the scientific facts behind every phenomenon; and he had a lot of questions to ask. He often asked why the waves lash, why the sun sets, why you cannot look at the midday sun, why the water boils, and many more. The delicate mind was taking a shape now.

Azad vividly remembers that despite financial constraints in the family, as a child, all of his necessities were provided for in terms of food, medicine or clothes. Thus, enjoying a secure childhood under the affectionate and watchful eyes of his parents, Azad started to grow learning from different sources. He is very reminiscent of his mother, who cooked for several people daily and fed them with love. He often ate with her, who served the rice mixed with aromatic *sambar* on a banana leaf, together with a variety of home-made pickles and coconut *chutney*. No food is tastier than the food your mother cooks, felt Dr. Kalam. This is true of everybody.

All his life, Dr. Kalam recalled how lovely his mother was. One day, during the Second World War days, when the food was in a short supply and only limited food was available for everybody to eat, his mother baked *chapattis* instead of rice. The child Azad sat with other siblings and kept eating; he was tired and hungry after a long spell of play, little realising that he had eaten his mother's share too. He realised his folly only when his elder brother pulled him up and explained that there was just enough for everybody to eat, two-three *chapattis* each. His voice was stern, "Amma will never say 'No' to you, but because you kept eating, she kept serving you, and tonight she will go hungry…"

It was a moment of shame, but it also gave him a vital lesson: You couldn't afford to forget the needs of those around you.

Azad was one of the ten siblings in his large family. As a small child, he never had any moment of boredom as he had the company of cousins and children of distant relatives in addition to his own brothers and sisters to play with. Of all, Azad was closer to Zohra, one of the older children in the family. She went to school and also did her share in the household duties, helping the mother in cooking and cleaning. She too was like a motherly figure for Azad, because he was a bit of a dreamer in his childhood even; he did not like to engage himself in boisterous activities or planning a prank like other boys; he would often curl up with a book or paper, and Zohra ensured that he was not disturbed or none of his needs went unattended.

Azad accompanied his father, Jainulabdeen to the old mosque in the locality for the evening prayers. The child did not understand the prayers as they were in the Arabic, but he was sure that 'they reached God'. His father had an element of divine touch, and it was due to this that when his father came out of the mosque, people from different religions waited for him with bowls of water. His father would dip his fingertips in them and say a prayer. This water was meant for the invalids. He remembered that many people visited his father thanking for the cure, who attributed this to the kind benevolence of God.

The environment in which Azad grew was replete with spirituality. His inquisitive mind had so many questions to ask in different realms of life, and spirituality was no exception. One day, he asked his father, who sat in the company of Pakshi Lakshamana Sastry, about the relevance of prayer. His father said that prayer helps a person transcend his body and become a part of the cosmos, all types of worldly divisions become irrelevant. Such simple explanations of the complex ideas helped the child understand spirituality in its right perspective. He learnt that man is a human being first: 'every human being is a specific element within the whole of the manifest divine being'. Azad saw people take water for the invalids, but its explanation from his father rooted his mind in scientific spirituality, when his father said that human beings, when confronted with problems, look for company and saviour; they came to him for water as they saw him as a go-between them and the Divine, but it was not at all a right thing to do. He advised him to distinguish between the fear-ridden vision of destiny and the vision of Supreme Bliss that resides within every human being. Until the last, Dr. Kalam continued to feel convinced that there exists a divine power that can help overcome all confusion and misery, and guide him to the true place. Adding to it, he advises that one has to only sever his emotional and physical bond to find himself treading on the path to freedom, ultimately leading to happiness and peace of mind.

Ahmed Jallaluddin too helped the child Azad shape his spiritual ideas. The two came into the contact when Jainulabdeen embarked on the project of building a wooden sailboat to take pilgrims from Rameswaram to Dhanuskodi and back. Jallaluddin was older than Azad by about fifteen years, but the two grew close to each other. It was, in fact, he who started to call the child Azad. They often used their free time walking along the street and on the seashore, and their discussion seemed part of the wider arrangement of

Early Life

things because spirituality reigned supreme in the environment. As they passed by the temple of Lord Shiva, circling round it like faithful devotees, they felt a flow of energy pass through them. The child had many questions to ask about God, and Jallaluddin answered them all. The child believed, in true spirit, that the prayers of the pilgrims, who took bath in the sea and chanted devotedly, also reached the same formless God, as did the prayers from the mosque. This convinced him that all religions were essentially the same, just different ways to pray and reach the same Entity.

People often want their dreams realised, and if they cannot realise them themselves, want others to realise them. Something of the sort happened with Jallaluddin. He could not go beyond schooling because of financial constraints in the family, and he wanted that Azad should excel in studies. He encouraged him to study harder, learn things better and did his bit to tell of the things around and beyond. In fact, Jallaluddin was the only person on the entire island who could write English; people came to him to get their letters written and read. He was always there to serve others, especially Azad who learnt different shades of life from him. It was he who introduced the child with new inventions, discoveries, medical science, education and many more things. He was like an important annexure to his school education. Azad asked him the questions which could not be satisfied in school. He kept asking him about the clouds, the rain, the train engines and the waves, and Jallaluddin kept answering him patiently. When he did not know something, he said it so, and tried to find answers to his questions from other sources like newspapers.

First Income

The child Azad was also greatly influenced by Samsuddin, his first cousin. He ran a newspaper agency and was the only distributor in Rameswaram. He worked alone to fetch the newspapers from the railway station in the morning and distribute them all over the town to meet the needs of about 1,000-strong literate community. The print media was, in essence, the only source of information about the news from across the country and world. The *Dinamani* was the most widely read paper in town. Azad often saw people sit in groups and discuss different news stories hotly; their topics varied from the current freedom movement to the holocaust that was likely to engulf the world soon. Azad was yet to learn to read, so he formed his own ideas from the words that he heard from others. For him, Samsuddin knew everything.

When the Second World War broke out in 1939, it became extremely difficult for Samsuddin to manage his business alone. The British were involved in the war right since the beginning, and they declared India a party to the war. Azad was only eight years old, and he did not understand why the demand for tamarind seeds had shot up suddenly and what this had to do with the war. A local fallout of the war was that the train halt at Rameswaram was suspended, which simply meant that Samsuddin could no more fetch newspapers. Will his business collapse with this? He thought out and found a way out. He could continue with his business if he had a helping hand; and somehow, he found Azad who could fill the slot well. Now, the newspapers were bundled and thrown out from the moving train on the Rameswaram Road, that was situated between Rameswaram and Dhanuskodi. Azad picked up the bundles and kept them until Samsuddin returned to finally distribute them. It was how the child earned his first wages. Dr. Kalam felt the 'surge of pride' of having earned his first income. He also earned some money gathering tamarind seeds and selling them to the nearby provisions store.

And this new venture made Azad all the busier. His day began early, well before dawn. All day, he was busy with his Koran class, newspaper delivery and school: all these brought him back home only in the evening to find

Early Life

himself in the comforting ways of his mother and grandmother. His mother ensured that Azad faced no difficulty. She often fed him part of her share even, and when Azad pointed it out, she would say that she was doing what was needed for him. She summed up what any mother could have done, but she was special, when she said, "This is what mothers look out for, don't worry about me." She was very sentimental that a little boy had to work so hard all day. As the tired Azad slept, she would sit by him to caress her hair, and often tears would roll down her cheeks. She found solace in the little accomplishments that the family achieved, she never thought an iota about herself. Her way of working had a lesson for the little Azad: No matter how small or large your sphere of activity is, what is of utmost importance is your commitment. With this quality, you can raise the level of any work to its highest glory.

Azad was growing up with so many influences from different quarters of life: mother, father, school, community and, of course, the most prominent were Jallaluddin and Samsuddin, that his personality became multidimensional. Dr. Kalam admits that it was their company that made all the difference in his later life. He attributes his creativity to these two geniuses who found ways for every problem they faced. And then, there were more influences waiting for him in his childhood.

You have to face confrontation and opposition when you set out to do something that is considered against the set ideals and orthodox living. That was what the child Azad went through when he was first invited by his science teacher Sivasubramania Iyer, a high-caste Brahmin to dine with him at his home. He had seen promise in Azad and wanted him to develop 'at par with the highly educated people of the cities'. His wife, however, was an orthodox lady. How could she bear with a Muslim boy dining in her 'ritually pure' kitchen? Sivasubramania Iyer knew it could well happen, and he was ready for this. He served the child with his own hands, not only this, he sat beside him and ate, while his wife watched the two from a distance. Azad wondered if there was any difference between the way the two ate, drank water or cleaned the floor after the meal. The doting teacher invited him to visit his house again for a meal, and when Azad hesitated, he said that such things were bound to happen when you set to change the system. Such opposition could not be made a stumbling block in the path of progress and modernisation. He was not wrong either. Next time, when Azad visited his teacher, his wife herself took him inside the kitchen and served him food with her own hands. To change the system, you need not break it, you have to just mould and moderate it, and that the teacher had done so perfectly; and it was a lesson of the lifetime for the delicate mind.

Dr. Kalam has vivid memories of his school life. He has learnt from his primary school, where he studied from 1936 to 1944 that it is the teacher with love, rather than a school with a magnificent building or great facilities or great advertisements, who can change the life of children the most. He recalls that the building of his school, the Rameswaram Panchayat Primary School, the only school in town then, had a brick structure with a thatched roof, but he does not remember even if a student ever dropped out. The teachers cared for every student, and took personal interest in their development. The teachers wanted them all not only to score good marks, but also to become good human beings, and to develop a love for the subjects that they taught.

Today, most schools have prescribed uniforms for students, it was not so in Azad's school. Children were free to wear what they felt like, and mostly, students wore their traditional dresses. His friend, Ramanadhan sported a tuft like his father, while Azad himself wore a little woven skullcap, like many Muslim boys of the town. But such distinctions did not mean anything to anyone there; they all seemed part of the grand harmonious system, in which each

Early Life

distinction was like a shade in the rainbow, each of it contributing to make it majestic. If anyone tried to disturb this rainbow, he was opposed, because maintaining harmony is the responsibility of everybody. Azad too experienced such a case when an attempt was made to disturb this harmony.

Azad was in the third standard when a new teacher was appointed. He too was a Hindu Brahmin. As soon as he came to the class and cast a quick appraising eye over all students, who sat there in their respective traditional dresses, and there was something that was like a shock to him. He overlooked the bright eyes of the students, and rather focussed his gaze at the front bench where Azad and Ramanadhan shared the desk. The two boys felt uncomfortable at the sharp gaze that pierced through their bodies. The teacher came close to Azad and demanded to know his name, and in response to the reply, he ordered him to stand up, gather his things and shift to the back row.

Azad stood rooted to the ground, humiliated and desperate, but he could not do anything. It was a brazen attempt to shatter the harmony that had prevailed in the town for ages. He moved back with his teary eyes. Before he moved, he looked at his partner, Ramanadhan who too had tears in the eyes. They could not oppose what their teacher had ordered; but once at home, they promptly narrated to their parents what had happened at school. Their fathers were equally shocked, because it had belied their faith in harmony. The two mild-mannered men felt agitated, met and discussed what had transpired at school. The two holy men were joined by the third holy man of the town, Father Bodal. The three decided that they could not allow the town to be thrown in the tumultuous state of discord that prevailed in other parts of the country, they could not allow the fabric of the town to be torn in any way. With dignity and courtesy, rooted in firmness, they apprised the new teacher how his minor action had gone on to divide the young minds and to inflict the society with divisiveness. The teacher realised his folly, begged sorry for his action and rectified the wrong he had committed.

This incident has a lesson for all of us. Effort has to be made to establish harmony and coherence in the society; these words have to be infused with the spirit of liveliness with our constant care and focus. Dr. Kalam states that he learnt from this incident that dialogue remains the most adequate tool to settle differences; blaming others for their shortcomings can only worsen the matter. This was the kind of environment in which he lived his childhood.

His belief in science was further strengthened by spirituality that he learnt in the company of the three holy men in the town, and it was owing to this amalgamation that he found himself well-versed with holy texts from different religions: the Koran, the Gita and the Bible. This is the spirit that makes India a true multi-religious, multi-ethnic nation, that provides a space for members of each community. He advises solemnly that there will always be attempts by vested interests to shatter the harmonious peace, and it should be confronted by bringing out the deeds of those people who have worked to strengthen the bond between communities. Unfortunately, the media gives more space to the forces that are out to destroy peace, and positive news seldom makes it to the front page or prime news. Until his end, Dr. Kalam continued to believe that India will, 'continue to survive and thrive as a secular democracy forever'.

◻

3
The First Step

The national life was passing through a transition under the leadership of Mahatma Gandhi, guided by truth, fearlessness and compassion; and this was the time for the child Azad to step out of the comfort zone of his house and town and enter the world, with the early influences he had received until now. To cap all of them, his father allowed him to go and attain glory. He had to go away to grow. The nest is comfortable for the seagull, but still it leaves it to put its wings to test and learn. The child Azad was now entering adolescence, the period of life described as the most restless part. His father wished him to nurse fathomless dreams and endeavour to realise them. He freed the young mind from the family bonds and said that he was the son of Life's longing for itself. You learn from others but you have to cultivate your thoughts, and this was what his father advised him.

As Jainulabdeen waved to bid him farewell at the railway station, Abdul Kalam travelled to Ramnathpuram in the company of his role models until then, Samsuddin and Jallaluddin. There, he was enrolled in the Schwartz High School. Abdul found himself in a completely new environment. It was a thriving town, but it lacked the essence of Rameswaram rooted in harmony and coherence. Feeling homesick in the initial period, Abdul realised that he had to come to terms with the new setting; returning to hometown could not lead him to realise his dreams, which were exalted though still vague. When you are on the path to realise your dreams, you cannot lie in the comfort zone; you have to tread in the unknown, strange world to create a niche for yourself. The more he thought about his hometown, the farther he was destined to be swept away from there. His father wanted him to be a Collector, and he set down to see how he could realise this dream of his father. The power of positive thinking, inculcated in him by Jallaluddin, helped him during the bouts of homesickness.

Azad missed his mother the most; she was a religious lady offering her prayers faithfully and serving the family with the best she could do. She stood by his father through thick and thin, making do with the limited income that the household earned from coconut groves and ferry business; their basic needs were being met, but they could not afford to indulge themselves in luxuries. She looked the image of peacefulness during her prayers as well as at other times; she never lost her temper despite the fact that she had to feed the large family, in addition, several people often dropped in, and she had never a word of complaint. At the top of that, she cooked a delicious food. She was adept at this art so well that she could bring out the aroma of each spice in her dishes.

Azad missed even his school teachers at Rameswaram, for whom students were part of the extended family, they took personal care of each student. The teachers at the Schwartz were refined and more knowledgeable, and very earnest to their duty, but the personal touch was missing for the most part. However, as Jallaluddin had taught him, there are two ways in which you can feel at ease in the world: either adapt yourself to the environment around you, or mould the environment to suit you. Azad was not yet in a condition to adopt the latter, so he chose the former. He had to, he could not undermine the high hopes that his father, his family and Jallaluddin had reposed in him.

The First Step

Azad soon found a way out how to overcome his homesickness when he grew a rapport with Manickam, a nationalist revolutionary. His house at Ramanathpuram was a treasure trove of books, and he graciously loaned books to Azad. It was during the course of his reading a number of books that he came across *The Laws of Success*, written by Napoleon Hill, a celebrated American writer. This book had profound effect on his psyche, and there were several statements that he wanted to read and read again.

Azad had lived his childhood in the affectionate ways of his parents, who sacrificed their own comforts to meet the needs of the children in the best way they could. When during the Second World War, the food was rationed and there was a general shortage of nearly everything, his mother often ate less so that the children had their fill. He also remembered his sister, Zohra who had come to his aid on many occasions, but she was still to make her greatest contribution in Azad's life, and the opportunity came a little too soon.

While Azad was studying at Ramanathpuram, Jallaluddin married Zohra. After schooling, Azad wanted to study engineering at the Madras Institute of Technology (MIT), but finance was a big hurdle. Zohra ensured that his dreams were fulfilled, and Jallaluddin motivated her to do her bit. It was not bit, it was a step that changed the very course of life for Azad. He needed to deposit a princely sum of Rs. 600 for admission to the MIT. This sum might look small today, but it was a big amount those days. His sister came to his rescue. The husband and wife discussed, and she, without a moment's thought, mortgaged her jewellery with a moneylender to manage the sum needed for his admission. It was an overwhelming gesture on her part as she too barely managed her household and this gold could have stood by her during hard times, but she was ready to do anything to see her brother nurture into a giant personality. She had faith in his abilities, and Jallaluddin supported her action.

Azad reciprocated the action by studying hard and saving on every penny during his graduation, and earned a scholarship to repay the money, but could he repay the gratitude? Dr. Kalam felt indebted to her all his life: that was perhaps the greatest tribute to her.

Dreams Make Life

Azad felt convinced that dreams are there to be achieved. He was motivated by the idea that 'dreams are not to be had during sleep, they are to be conceived when awake', and this was the idea that he continued to teach to the young. The dreams that you see can be realised, they are like a seed from which can blossom a massive tree. Knowing the value of dreams, he was on the path to dream; he judged the dreams that his father had and those that he himself had, and he had to come to terms with them. His own dreams were at variance with those of his father, who wanted him to be a Collector. His teacher at Schwartz, Iyadurai Solomon identified the genius residing in the young student, and he started to tend him. He told his students to realise their dreams in the context of the national reality. He wanted them to excel in their fields, but at the same time, also take stock of the prevailing situation. The fact was that the prevailing situation was quite perturbing at that time. The Quit India Movement in 1942 had galvanised the British into conceding freedom for the country, but it had unprecedented outcome in the form of communal tensions. The situation in some border towns was very volatile, where a large number of deaths occurred. Azad could not imagine that a neighbour could kill a neighbour. He had learnt that neighbours are part of the extended family, but it was not the case all over the country. Freedom came in 1947 after partition of the country into two, but the communal riots had marred the jubilation and celebration. It was simply an abuse of the newly-gained freedom.

Freedom brought in more challenges and it was here that the growing young mind had a vital role to play. Azad was now bracing himself to create a role for himself; yet he was undecided.

Failures are stepping stones to success; if taken in a positive sense, they can prove very helpful in carving the future course of action. Kalam himself advises, "I firmly believe that unless one has tasted the bitter pill of failure, one cannot aspire enough for success." He himself tasted failure on some occasions, but he did not sit back. He tasted his first failure when he was a student of aeronautics at the MIT.

Prof. Srinivasan, his design teacher as well as the head of the institute, formed teams of four students each, and Kalam's team was required to design a low-level attack aircraft. In his team, Kalam was assigned to make the aerodynamic design. As he was wont to, he and his team worked hard on different aspects of the system and put in long hours of hard work. The professor too kept an eye on his progress. One day, the professor came to his room and demanded to see the progress. On seeing the diagram Kalam had made, his eyebrows crinkled up and warned, "Kalam, this stands nowhere in terms of design and thought, I am disappointed." The professor went away leaving Kalam desperate and disappointed, but not without having ordered him to remake the entire design, and he allowed mere three days for it. He was stunned at what his professor had said. In fact, this was the first time that any teacher had censured his work. It was a little setback for him, but, at the same time, it was a new experience. It was a challenge, and failure in this challenge could mean his scholarship being stopped; his entire education was at stake, and could not allow it to happen at any cost. The dreams of his parents, his sister,

Jallaluddin and teachers could have been shattered, in addition to destroying his own ambitions, his own dreams.

Kalam overcame his disappointment and set down to work, determined to prove himself. He skipped his dinner and worked at the drawing board through the night. Dreams cannot be allowed to remain dreams, they have to be realised on the hard ground, and for it hard work is needed which Kalam was ready to put in. He considered all options with the design, thought about in various ways, and when he saw the sky getting red at dawn, his mind was flooding with new ideas. He now knew what he had to do. In two days, Kalam was nearing the completion of his design, and he was sure that the design would meet his professor's expectations. It was a Sunday evening, and Kalam stood from his chair to straighten his stiff back; as he turned, he found his professor standing before himself. He never knew how long the professor had been there. He wished him, who once again demanded to see the drawing. He looked at the design critically, and then hugged him, uttering a word that could explain his sentiments: 'Outstanding!'

Before the professor left, he said that he knew the time of three days was very short, in fact, not enough to complete the work, yet Kalam had emerged with flying colours. This must be realised that this is the only way dreams can be realised, and he did everything that was possible under the circumstances.

Overcoming the obstacle through hard work and thinking taught Kalam a lesson of the lifetime. This experience was to stand in good stead in the times to come when he would be assigned the responsibilities of designing satellites and missiles.

The stay at the MIT was also instructive in other aspects, as shades of his personality came to the fore when Kalam took part in other fields. Tamil, his mother tongue, is an ancient and classical language of India, enriched by a large volume of literature. The MIT Tamil Sangam (a literary club) organised an essay competition, in which he contributed with an article 'Let Us Make Our Own Aircraft'. He won the first prize, thus giving him a first-hand experience on writing.

The life at the MIT was very exciting, and it became all the more exciting with the touching treatment that Kalam received from Prof. Sponder. In the farewell party, all the graduating students had lined up in three rows with the professors seated in the front row. As the cameraman set his focus, Prof. Sponder stood up and looked around. Seeing Kalam standing in the third row, he called, "Come and sit with me in the front." It was an amazing invitation. Kalam hesitated, but Prof. Sponder continued, "You are my best student, and you will sure bring glory to your teachers in the future." When the young engineer took leave of his professor, he was blessed in emotional words, "Let God Himself enlighten your path into the future."

□

4
Failure is a Stepping Stone

After Kalam obtained his degree at the MIT, he went to work with the HAL (Hindustan Aeronautics Limited), Bengaluru as a trainee. Working in a team on aircraft, their design and technology, especially engine overhauling, he thought about his career. This practical experience was very educative. It seemed as if the theoretical aspect of his learning was making a rendezvous with practical wisdom, giving him a strange sense of excitement. He learnt valuable lessons in the working principle of 'after-burning' of gas dynamics and diffusion processes; he also gained valuable experience in radial engine-cum-drum operations. There were many other operations that he learnt there. And one of the most important lessons for him was to know the importance of technicians who contributed in the success of any project like an inevitable tool; they might not have studied in major universities, but the hands-on experience over years had turned them all into vital factors of any project.

Kalam had two options before him: to start his career as an engineer and as a pilot. He weighed his options and decided in the favour of flying as a career. Having become a graduate aeronautical engineer from the HAL, he applied to the IAF (Indian Air Force) for a flying job, and also to the DTD&P (Directorate of Technical Development and Production – Air), the Ministry of Defence. He received calls for interview from both. The former was to be held at AFSB (Air Force Selection Board), Dehradun while the latter was to be held at New Delhi. The journey from a little-known town to north India was a long one geographically; the long time it took, gave him time to think about his options. He had first seen an aircraft at the MIT where two decommissioned aircraft had been kept for demonstration of various subsystems to the students. These demonstrations had taken Kalam's aspiration with a storm, and he dreamt of flying. For him, flying was not to be a career, rather it meant to him a man's ability to think beyond his boundaries, where new zeniths of success could be tasted and new milestones created.

The journey over 2,000 km had a vital lesson for Kalam. He had only read in his textbooks how vast his country is, but he saw it unfolding before his eyes. He saw the lifestyles, dressing styles, eating styles and speaking styles undergo a change as the train covered long distances. His motherland seemed to uncover herself before him like a fleeting view of panorama. He was proud of his country, and this experience convinced him that his motherland demanded of him to work as hard as he could so that its people could overcome their misery and enter a new era of modern living. The charm of countryside was simply majestic, like a spell on his psyche. He now loved his country even more intensely.

The interview at the DTD&P (Air) had to be conducted first, so he stopped at New Delhi for a week. The interview was conducted in favourable circumstances, and he hoped to get success. His education at Schwartz and MIT had helped to develop his personality too. He was no more a shy, hesitant boy that he had been when he left Rameswaram for the first time; he was now a confident young man in his early twenties with an ability to articulate his thoughts in English and Tamil well enough.

The interview at the SSBs (these include AFSBs) by which commissioned officers are selected for training in different armed forces, is special in its nature. It is conducted over four-five days and lays more stress on personality rather than knowledge, on qualities rather than smartness. It conducts a variety of tests, such as picture description test, apperception test, lecturette, GTO tests and face-to-face interview among other things to finally select the candidates. Kalam did as well as he could, and secured the ninth position. Unfortunately, or fortunately, only eight vacancies were available, so he could not be selected, and with this, his dream of becoming a pilot was shattered.

The result of the SSB interviews was announced on the final day of the interview. Rejection brings despair and emptiness, which Kalam too faced. But who knew what lay in store for him? Maybe, the IAF had lost a genius, but it was a gain for the country and world, as the later developments would prove. For now, feeling desperate and forlorn, Kalam walked out of the AFSB. He wanted some peace of mind. He knew it hard to tell to his parents that he could not make it. He did not want to give them any unfavourable news. He needed to think over his career afresh and to rearrange his priorities. He needed some solitude, so he headed to Rishikesh.

Motivation

Kalam reached Rishikesh in the morning hours. He was mesmerised by the vastness and cleanliness of the Ganga with the holy surroundings, in the lap of picturesque hills around. He took a dip. Its cold water soothed his turbulent mind. He sat in the water for quite some time, little caring for the belongings he had left on the cemented bank. When he felt a little relieved, he came out, wiped his body, wore his clothes, and then walked to the Sivananda Ashram, located a little way up a hill.

Tranquillity and energy seemed to engulf Kalam when he entered the serene atmosphere in the Ashram. He felt as if peace had dawned on him, he did not know why he felt joyful, despite the setback he had just faced the previous day. In his hometown, he had often seen pilgrims and *sadhus* perform rituals; here he found many meditating. He looked around and queried if he could get answers to the questions that perturbed his mind. He was sure he could get his answers here. The head of the Ashram, Sivananda himself welcomed him.

"What troubles you?" asked the tranquil Sivananda as if he knew the fact, while Kalam wondered how he could know about his desperate mind; what amazed him more was that his being a Muslim did not matter anything; for him an innocent young boy stood before him. Kalam was thinking what to say when Sivananda said again, "What troubles you, my child?"

Kalam felt he was in the presence of someone before whom he could lay bare his heart. He narrated to the seer his background, his education, his dreams and his failures. The seer listened to each of his words carefully and calmly.

What Sivananda advised put Kalam on a path that was predestined for him. Let us listen these words from the mouth of Dr. Kalam: "Accept your destiny and go ahead with your life. You are not destined to become an air force pilot. What you are destined to become is not revealed now, but it is predetermined. Forget this failure, as it was essential to lead you to your destined path. Search, instead, for the true purpose of your existence...Surrender yourself to the wishes of God."

These words were prophetic for Kalam; his way of thinking underwent a change. He was confident that his failure at Dehradun was part of a larger arrangement of things which he could not understand at that juncture. He accepted that he could no more chase to be an air force pilot. He returned to New Delhi with a positive energy flowing in his veins. There, he found that he had been selected as a senior scientific assistant at the DTD&P. With this, his career started on a positive note, and the time to come was to reveal what Destiny wished of him. Let us tell you that Kalam could not be a pilot, nonetheless, his desire to fly a supersonic aircraft was fulfilled later in life. We will tell you how in the coming pages of the book.

□

5
Working Life

The year was 1958. Kalam returned to Delhi and visited the DTD&P (Air); in response to his query about the interview, he was handed over the appointment letter. The very next day, he joined as a senior scientific assistant. He trusted what Sivananda had said. He accepted this job as his destiny, and set down to work as well as he could. He gave up his ambition to be an air force pilot. Though he was not directly involved in flying, he was very much involved in helping people to fly as his initial posting was at the Technical Centre (Civil Aviation), where he worked on assessment of aircraft designs. He also had a stint of carrying out a design assignment on a supersonic target aircraft under the leadership of his director, Dr. Neelakantan.

Kalam's competence was praised, so to gain further experience, he was sent to the Aircraft and Armament Testing Unit (A&ATU), Kanpur to work in a tropical evaluation of Gnat Mk I aircraft. There, he participated in the performance assessment of its operation systems. Living in Kanpur was a new experience for him. It was a populous city. Crowded and noisy streets seemed to prevail everywhere. The morning time was a little restless when mist mixed with industrial smoke made breathing hard. Moreover, it was not easy to get what he was used to eat. He felt alone in this crowd, so he engaged himself in his work wholeheartedly. He also observed how people had left their caring families to work in factories at low wages, and it was like a new revelation of the industrial and city life.

Kalam returned to Delhi to take up his next assignment, and this time, he was a member of the design team assigned with the design of a DART target. After successful completion of this project, he seemed to have created a niche for himself. He was now being given important assignments, including a preliminary design study on a human centrifuge, vertical take-off and landing platform design, hot cockpit design and others. As his skills improved, he was thought fit to be posted to the ADE (Aeronautical Development Establishment), which was set up at Bangalore (now Bengaluru).

The new environs in Bangalore were quite in contrast with those of Delhi or Kanpur. Kalam minutely observed. As he worked on different projects, he passed his evening going round the streets, gardens and shopping plazas in the city, observing people with a keen eye. His observation was quite interesting. He concluded that people had cultivated extreme traits owing to different masters that they had been subjected to in the past. Moreover, the pressures of work had compelled people to migrate from one place to another, and with it, a change in their masters occurred. This change brought about a blend of cultures. This also cultivated contrasting qualities in people. As they were loyal to different masters at different times, they were possessed of two opposite qualities in the same extreme. He saw that people could be very compassionate and cruel at the same time; so was the case with other qualities like laziness and perseverance, sensitiveness and indifference, deepness and fickleness. In old Delhi, he had seen people still being influenced by the ways of the Mughals when they walked in the streets of Chandni Chowk looking for a variety of Mughal cuisines; while in New Delhi, a new western world was coming to the fore, imitating ways of the British. The people in Kanpur were quite in contrast, still imitating the *paan*-chewing ways of Wazid Ali Shah. Even Bangalore seemed a world apart, he could not find a trace of the serene air of Rameswaram as he walked amongst the dog-walking Indians trying to look and behave like Europeans. His heart was in Rameswaram, but he had to focus his head in his workplace.

All this while, Kalam envisioned that his destiny had been chalking out his destiny, slowly but surely. As the ADE was a new establishment, he had to create preliminary facilities, and then he helped form a project team to design and develop an indigenous hovercraft prototype as a ground equipment machine (GEM). This was for the first time that he was assigned to lead the small team of four people, assigned with the job of completing the engineering project in three years' time. In fact, the project was the very initial vision of V.K. Krishna Menon, the then Defence Minister, by which he sought to produce defence equipment indigenously, so he himself took interest in it.

The idea was new and little literature or help was available. The team was yet inexperienced if judged from the standard of concepts. Moreover, none in the team had any experience to build a machine, let alone a flying machine. They tried to read as much literature as was available, but those were not the internet days, when most things could be available at the click of a mouse. They could not access any people who could guide or advise them. When they could not make much headway, Kalam finally decided to initiate the project on ground with the limited information and available resources.

A hovercraft is a vehicle that can travel just above the surface of water or land, held up by the air being forced downwards. As they set down to work on the project, new vistas opened up. Kalam compared it with an aircraft, and found several similarities between the two. He now knew that he would have to come to the best of his ingenuity; he remembered how the Wright brothers had made the first aeroplane after fixing bicycles! Working on the drawing board and hardware development room for a few months, Kalam had to seek his own opportunities. Though he led the team, yet his humble background confronted him with some unexpressed insubordination. He came from a small town, and hailed from a lower middle class family, not with any worthwhile family education to boast of. He knew he would have to prove his worth to command obedience; if he failed, he would have to retreat into a corner; this could mean endless struggle for creating a place for himself.

The team members joined heads to think, plan and make, part by part, one subsystem followed by another, and went from stage to stage. It was a new revelation. When you achieve a higher spectrum, your mind tends to fly still higher. But the people around did not have a favourable idea about the whole project, terming it an 'impossible' concept rooted in unrealistic principles. However, the Defence Minister and other superior officers seemed to be convinced that something could be done. Kalam worked wholeheartedly, often he worked overtime, he wanted the project to see the light of the day; it would have established him as an inventor. Withstanding criticism like 'eccentric' and 'navvy', he led his team with a mission in the mind. Whenever he confronted criticism, he recalled John Trowbridge's well-known satirical poem on the Wright brothers, published in 1896, see how it went:

> ...*with thimble and thread*
> *And wax and hammer, and buckles and screws,*
> *And all such things as geniuses use;*
> *Two bats for patterns, curious fellows!*
> *A charcoal-pot and a pair of bellows.*

Despite criticism, the Wright brothers had created history, and Kalam was himself on the course of creating history...nay histories in the times to come.

In a year's time, the untiring efforts led to bringing into existence several subsystems and a basic model which could lead to take the shape of a hovercraft. The director and the Defence Minister were delighted at the progress, and appreciated the effort. It was the stage when the GEM machine was christened Nandi, after the bull mount of Lord Shiva. As the establishment lacked facilities to give a final shape to its external form, they had no chance of finishing it, but it was certainly a prototype to fly with.

The Defence Minister himself wanted to fly in the Nandi, but the accompanying officials were concerned with his safety, but he had trust in the capability and competence of the engineers. "Let us go for a ride," said the minister.

"Yes, Sir," said Kalam with a confident air about him. He went forward and occupied the small cockpit, while the minister sat beside him. There was a group captain in the minister's troupe, with a long flying experience. He might have no doubts about the machine, but he certainly had doubts about the flying abilities of the engineer in the cockpit, and he being an air force pilot, was much confident of his own capabilities. Moreover, he could not take chances with the life of his Defence Minister, as he felt that he could manage any emergencies that might be faced in the nascent machine. So, he gestured to Kalam to come out of the machine. Kalam looked direct into his eyes and shook his eyes in the negative, murmuring to himself, "I am sure about my competence in flying the machine."

The Defence Minister himself was on the side of Kalam. He gave a hearty laugh and asked Kalam to start the machine and move. He was happy with the way the machine performed. He said that they had to open up further vistas to look for more powerful, bigger machines in the times to come. The group captain too heaved a great sigh of relief when the machine touched down safely.

The project was completed ahead of its schedule successfully. However, Kalam came across a new realisation.

Working Life

The success of a project depends not only on the competence of engineers and technicians, it also involves capable decisions at the bureaucratic and political levels. Krishna Menon had foreseen the military applications of the hovercraft, so he wanted its further development, but by the time the project was completed, he had quit the office and could not pursue the project any further. The people replacing him did not see any wisdom in the project. It is true that the project was in its very initial stage, but this is the way progress is made. If we see in the nearer past, we find that the LCA (Light Combat Aircraft) took as many as thirty years to complete, with some obstacles still persisting. Casting away the indigenous hovercraft could not be called a wise step, however, it did happen. The fact remains that India continues to import hovercrafts. Had it developed one of its own, India would have been self-dependent in this field, rather it might have led to earning valuable foreign currency, as it has happened with our space flights.

Casting away the project of Nandi was like a personal loss to Kalam; it was like a failure that had been attributed to him, despite the shower of praise that he received. He felt disappointed and disillusioned. He needed motivation at this stage. When he had tasted failure at Dehradun, he had sought the blessings of Sivananda; this time he looked around, but finding none to help and guide him, he looked to his childhood. He recalled the words of Pakshi Sastry, "Seek the truth and the truth shall set you free." As soon as he remembered this, he strengthened his mind and looked forward to more challenges. The opportunity came too soon.

Kalam was in his cabin thinking over how the hovercraft could be further improved despite the fact that the project had been shelved for now. The hovercraft seemed to bring a ray of hope for him, when Dr. Mendiratta, his director, sent for him. Kalam entered his office, wished him and sat down. The director enquired if he was in the right set of mind. Kalam nodded in the affirmative, hiding his sentiments. "And what about the hovercraft?" the director asked.

"It is in a perfect condition, it can be flown at any moment," Kalam asserted.

"Well, then, get the machine ready for a demonstration, an important visitor is likely tomorrow," said the director.

Kalam's face glowed up. It could mean some positive news, he thought and he hurriedly went back, called his technicians and supervised to prepare the hovercraft for the following day. Still he wondered in his mind who that important visitor could be; so far as he knew, no VIP was scheduled to visit the establishment over the next week.

The next day, Kalam stood near the hovercraft and waited for the important person. Soon, Dr. Mendiratta accompanied a handsome, tall and bearded man. The man seemed to possess a wide scientific knowledge. He asked some very penetrating questions, and with each of Kalam's answers, his face displayed an expression of appreciation. When he had asked all his questions, he turned to Dr. Mendiratta and said, "Let's go." And then he turned again and said to Kalam, "Can you give me a ride in it?"

Kalam was greatly encouraged at this demand. He joyfully nodded. Destiny was coming closer, he felt. He flew the machine just a few centimeters above the ground as they went round the complex for over ten minutes. The visitor had many more questions, and they were adequately answered. When he got down, he shook Kalam's hand and said, "Congratulations."

It was at this juncture that he divulged his identity. He was none other than Prof. MGK Menon, Director TIFR (Tata Institute of Fundamental Research). It was for the first time that Kalam had met him, though he had heard about him before too.

Not many days later, Kalam received a call for interview from the INCOSPAR (Indian Committee for Space Research); it was a procedure to select him as a rocket engineer. This agency, located at Bombay (now Mumbai) was responsible for conducting space research in the country.

Kalam did not have much time to prepare, nor did he know what type of questions could be posed to him. He once again looked to his childhood guide, Lakshamana Sastry who had once told him that it was more important to hold faith in the Almighty than be immersed in delusion. The state of the mind is very important when you attempt to attain success. If you are tense and unconfident, success may brush past you; but when you are relaxed and free from doubt, success may be within an arm's distance, you have to just pluck it. Saying to himself that the best way to win was to 'not need to win'. He surrendered to his destiny, as he had no role in the visit of Prof. MGK Menon, which had culminated into this interview.

Kalam entered the interview room with freshness glowing on his face. His face shone still more brightly when he found across the table the legendary Dr. Vikram Sarabhai along with Prof. MGK Menon and Saraf, Deputy Secretary of the AEC (Atomic Energy Commission). The interview was held in complete harmony. It was aimed at finding out the possibilities that Kalam possessed, rather than knowledge and skills he possessed, so the interaction became all the more fruitful. As they explored deep into his psyche, their faces showed that they had struck at the right candidate for the job.

The following day, Kalam was informed that he had been selected as a rocket engineer and was to be absorbed in the INCOSPAR. This was like a dream come true.

□

6

The First Leap

Kalam's selection as a rocket engineer in the INCOSPAR was like starting to ascend the steps of a long-drawn destined path; it was like stepping on the ladder to success for the first time. What made him jubilant at the place was the working atmosphere. Your rank and level did not matter much, what mattered was performance, unlike the bureaucratic and officialdom type of atmosphere at the DTD&P. The position at the INCOSPAR was like putting the satellite into its precise orbit. It made him confident that he would get to play a vital role in the national life. The professional type of atmosphere also prevailed at the TIFR Computer Centre, where he was sent for a familiarisation course. Everybody was part of the team, and even those were the vital members who 'stood and waited to serve'.

Confident of the talent the INCOSPAR possessed, it set out on an ambitious mission, that was to set up the TERLS (Thumba Equatorial Rocket Launching Station) at Thumba. At that time, it was a small sleeping fishing town, rather a village near Thiruvananthapuram in Kerala. The choice for the place was a difficult one and was part of the endeavour that Dr. Sarabhai and Dr. Bhabha made; it was Dr. Chitnis of the PRL (Physical Research Laboratory), Ahemedabad, who had spotted it and termed it suitable for the task. The reason for choosing it was its proximity to the earth's magnetic equator and the sea. The railway line passed on one side and the sea on the other. The only obstacle in acquiring it was a large church, named St. Mary Magadalene Church. Adjacent to it was also located the Bishop's house. As the experience goes in India, people tend to hold on to their even private lands and do not agree so readily to part with them even for nationally important projects, let alone smaller projects. The sentiments often run high when a religious structure is needed to build a project, and just this was the case here.

Dr. Sarabhai finally decided to speak to the Bishop, His Excellency Rev. Dr. Peter Bernard Pareira. The Bishop advised him to come the next day, a Sunday. In the morning mass, the Bishop addressed the congregation in his quiet and calm voice that there was a famous scientist with them. Dr. Sarabhai was a celebrated scientist even then. Everybody welcomed him with a roar of claps. The Bishop explained how science and spirituality were aimed at the same thing: science enriches human life, while spirituality leads to peace of the human mind. He said that what he himself and Dr. Sarabhai were doing was just the same; they both were working for human progress and prosperity; so they had to work in conjunction with each other. And in the end, he asked for their concurrence, "When his purpose is analogous to that of mine, should we not help him? He wants our church and the place I live for the work of space science and research. Can we give them God's abode for a scientific mission?"

Dr. Sarabhai waited with crossed fingers with earnest curiosity in his eyes, and his eyes brightened up when there was a hearty 'Amen' from those present there. The mission seemed to have been enriched by the divine blessing. This was how the first office of the Thumba Space Centre was housed in the church, its prayer room became Kalam's first laboratory, while the Bishop's room was made his design and drawing office. Till today, the church is maintained in the glory it deserves, and still houses the Indian Space

Museum. It is with the contribution of such exalted minds that a mission is taken forward. Something was being born which was destined to change the very future of the nation.

Potential has to be strengthened with skills, so Kalam was sent to the NASA (National Aeronautics and Space Administration) in the U.S. for a six-month-long training programme. Before he went abroad, he visited his hometown, informing his father and near and dear ones about the excellent opportunities he had in his hand. His father took him to the mosque for a thanksgiving namaz. The prayer has its spell, as it dawns peace on the mind, which leads to some tranquil moments giving rise to a flow of creativity. This is the reason that prayer is so important for a healthy living. Our subconscious is made up of ideas, potentials and abilities, dormant and distant, which the conscious wants to achieve, but which could not be realized somehow. In the words of Kalam, "Prayer helps us to tap and develop these powers."

It was an emotional farewell from the family members, as he was now set to fly to a mega city, New York. Coming from a mediocre town, he was now on his way to a civilization which calls itself the most advanced, at least in material terms.

At the NASA

Kalam was deputed for his training at the Langley Research Centre, Hampton, Virginia, under the NASA. It functions as a basic R&D centre for advanced aerospace technology.

At the NASA, Kalam visited different facilities dealing with different aspects of aerospace engineering, as Goddard Space Flight Centre, Greenbelt, Maryland and the Wallops Flight Facility at Wallops Island in East Coast, Virginia. At these facilities, Kalam learnt valuable lessons which could help him in the course of his career, but the conditions between two countries were poles apart, he knew, and those

The First Leap

working conditions could not be created back at home, so there was much room for innovation and creativity. He weighed his options if he would be able to match the giant nation of America in technology and know-how, if not in his lifetime, in the lifetime of the progeny.

In addition to his lessons in technology, Kalam also learnt from the things he observed. Two of these stood out, both of them being works of art. At Hampton, he saw a piece of sculpture in which a charioteer was driving two horses, one representing scientific research and the other technological development. This simply meant that research and development are intrinsically and inseparably interconnected. It was a useful lesson for him. The other was a painting depicting a battle scene with a few rockets flying in the background. You could hope for such paintings in a place which was dedicated to rocket science, but what caught his eye was the depiction of black soldiers, and not white soldiers; their features showed as if the soldiers hailed from South Asia. On close observation, he found that the painting depicted the battle between Tipu Sultan and the British, and the black soldiers were firing rockets. He stood before the painting for quite sometime wondering that the achievement of his people had been forgotten in his own country, while it was being commemorated on the other side of the planet. In fact, this has been the fact with we Indians. We are suffering from a sense of self-pity. We do not take pride in our ancient achievements. We do not know much about the Vedas that were created here in our land thousands of years ago, but we saw their wisdom only when the western scholars worked on them. Another example is that of Yog, now popularly called 'Yoga'. This ancient wisdom remained obscure in our own country, but became a popular concept after the western stamp. We discarded Yog but embraced Yoga, degrading our own wisdom. Something of the sort has happened with rocket science too. The west learnt about rocket science from our native craftsmen, but we do not know who developed this science. We allowed it to fall into oblivion. However, the west recognises its scientists who further developed it. We blame the westerners about having learnt from us, but is it not our own mistake that we discarded our ancient wisdom like garbage, only to shed crocodile tears? Kalam recognised that if the west has worked on our ancient ideas, we should not hesitate to work on the ideas they have developed, and give it a native colour.

Among other valuable lessons that Kalam learnt from this sojourn abroad can be summed up in a quotation from Benjamin Franklin: "Anything that hurts instructs." If you are faced with a problem, don't keep suffering from it, rather solve it head-on, and let it become a capability.

Kalam experienced a wide difference between the working styles in America and India. Often, our capabilities and potentials do not determine the jobs; the seniors think it below their standard to listen to their subordinates and people down the line. They hold a contemptuous attitude towards anyone who is not supposed to give out a bright idea; and if some bright idea is indeed brought out, credit is seldom given to its creator. This is the way Indian organisations are run. Rank hierarchy decides the level of wisdom, intelligence, capability and potential. This is the reason that the seniors tend to humiliate and disrespect those down the hierarchical order; and you cannot expect a subordinate to be creative and constructive if you humiliate him; he will, in that case, tend to do verbatim what a senior asks him to do.

Leadership is a tact, it has to be applied very understandably. A leader has to draw the fine line between two extremes: firmness and harshness, leadership and bullying, discipline and vindictiveness. The seniors who are able to distinguish between these two extremes, can hope to get the best out of their juniors. Kalam deplores that the line is rather drawn between 'heroes' and 'zeroes'; the former numbering only a few hundred, and the latter comprising the masses. This mindset has to be changed for the better. We cannot hope to become a developed country unless we change the situation on the ground. We have to give credit to those who have actually worked on a project, who have written a work and who deserve the award.

The First Rocket Launch

On his return from the NASA, Kalam started work on the Nike-Apache Rocket, made at the NASA. The lack of facilities is also a big question mark so far as operations in India are concerned. What they possessed to transport the rocket from the church building to the launch site and place it on the launch-pad included a truck and a manually-operated hydraulic crane. It was the minimum possible, and in case of any problem, they had no support to fall back upon. Kalam supervised the work of rocket integration and safety. He had to undertake the job of its launch on 21 November, 1963 with the help of two colleagues, D. Easwardas and R. Aravamudan; the former looking after rocket assembly and launch, and the latter was entrusted with the charge of radar, telemetry and ground support.

The first problem that they faced was when they lifted the rocket. It started to tilt to a side, suggesting that there was a leak in the hydraulic system of the crane. The time for the launch was fast approaching, which was 6 pm. There was no time to repair the crane; and this is where the team work came in. The entire team supported the rocket to finally place it on the launcher. Fortunately, the launch was smooth; and he completed the project successfully in terms of all the required functions. A sense of pride and accomplishment dawned on the team, but for Kalam, it was only a stopover, he was destined to do better and bigger things. He little rested in the glory of this achievement, and set his eyes on a higher target.

In 1960s, when this launch took place, India was still in its infancy so far as its rocket science was concerned, but so was not the case with the world. The US and the USSR possessed stockpiles of rockets and missiles, endangering the entire world. A crisis arose when the USSR built missile sites in Cuba from where it could launch missile attacks on several American cities. The US imposed a blockade barring the introduction of any offensive missiles to Cuba; not only this, it went forward with its plan to respond to any Soviet nuclear attack by retaliating against the USSR. The world shivered as the 'drama' unfolded and then subsided when the Soviet Union ordered the dismantling of the nuclear missile bases in Cuba. Russia was a patronising country for India, but in the future, there could be such a threat for India too; it may not be from these two countries, but it could well be from other countries. So, there was need to build up our own capabilities.

Kalam belonged to the next generation of engineers and scientists, who were to take over the job of taking forward rocket technology to further heights, under the capable leadership of Prof. Sarabhai. He was a luminary who believed not in degrees and grades in training, but in the skills and capabilities that an individual possessed. The success of the Nike-Apache Rocket, he divulged before his team of young scientists and engineers his dream of ascending to the next higher step, that was to build an Indian SLV (Satellite Launch Vehicle).

The world advances with the vision of a man like Prof. Sarabhai; he was willing to try out novel approaches and depend on younger generation. He often surprised his juniors when he advised them to do certain things, which appeared quite unrelated with the main work they were doing, but at a later time, it became an inseparable part of the entire project, such a seer he was! Prof. Sarabhai possessed fine judgement which made him extract the finest of his assistants; not only this, he was the guide who could predict when to stop or change the direction of innovation. He was an experimenter and innovator of the first degree.

Not only this, he was always available for any advice at any moment, whether he was available locally or not. He was leading a team of young and inexperienced, but nonetheless energetic and enthusiastic personnel who were set on a bigger target for themselves and for the nation, in the field of science and technology in general and in space research in particular. Whenever he visited Thumba, the people were electrified by his mere presence. They would work overtime willingly only to show something new. Their enthusiasm knew no limits. Innovation was taking place at the site in almost every sphere of the SLV, right from design to fabrication to even some administrative procedure.

While the work was still on this ambitious project, Prof. Sarabhai entrusted Kalam with a preliminary concept that seemed quite unrelated with the SLV. He asked him to start studying on a RATO (rocket-assisted take-off) system. This system was to be used in the military aircraft, and on the face of it, it had no connection with the SLV, except of course in the mind of this visionary. Kalam knew how the mind of this great man worked, so he welcomed the idea and invested his remaining energy on this concept. He knew that sooner or later an opportunity would come knocking at the door of his laboratory, and he could not allow it to slip away.

This was also the time when the rocket launch site at Thumba was developed into the TERLS (Thumba Equatorial Rocket Launch Station). It was done through active collaboration with France, the US and the USSR. The vision of Prof. Sarabhai was coming into reality. It was he who had trust in the Indian capability, though help from abroad had to be sought at least in the initial stages. Without him, it could have been quite a difficult task to achieve integrated national space programme. India was still in its initial stages so far as the making of equipment to manufacture the rockets and launch facilities was concerned, yet the main focus was on to develop indigenous capability. The missile, rocket and space programme in India in general and at Thumba in particular led to astonishing results. Work was started in multiple fields including scientific and technological development in rocket fuels, propulsion systems, aeronautics, aerospace materials, advanced fabrication techniques, rocket motor instrumentation, control and guidance systems, telemetry, tracking systems and scientific instruments for experimentation in space. As the work encompassed massive activity on the ground, potentials and capabilities started to be groomed and blossomed, and over the decades, some fine talent has emerged, which has made what India today is in the field of space technology.

I suppose it would be prudent to distinguish between different terms, especially a sounding rocket, a launch vehicle and a missile. All these are different kinds of rockets, manufactured to undertake different types of tasks. The (sounding) rockets are used for the near-earth missions, such as to probe a region, and can move up to the upper regions of the atmosphere; they can carry a variety of payloads to a range of altitudes for different tasks. Yet these rockets are not capable to impart the final velocity needed to orbit the payload. In contrast, a launch vehicle is designed to inject into orbit a technological payload or satellite. In its final stage, it provides necessary velocity to a satellite to be delivered into an orbit. It is a more complicated system than a rocket and requires onboard guidance and control systems, so that much of automation is achieved, though enabled by the tracking system on the ground. A missile is a further innovation of the previous two stages of space technology. In addition to the systems inbuilt in the previous two systems, it also has the capability to fine-tune its trajectory in terms of its target. If it is fired at an aircraft (which is a moving target), it is expected of a missile to change its direction to hit the target; thus it is inbuilt with target-tracking systems; and this is the reason that it has been inducted in military war equipment like never before.

The First Leap

The real journey of the Indian aerospace programme began with the RSR (Rohini Sounding Rocket). It raised India to a higher plane of technological innovation in space research. The initial rockets had low capability; the first Rohini rocket consisted of a single solid propulsion motor weighing a mere 32 kg, lifting a payload of a mere 7 kg to an altitude of about 10 km. With time, capability increased and precision achieved, and the subsequent rockets carried payloads weighing nearly 100 kg to an altitude of 350 km. But this was no time to sit back and relax, as the ante was further upped; much more was needed to be done.

The main point of these systems was indigenous element. With time, the indigenous contribution augmented, especially in the production of sounding rockets as well as their propellants. Work also started on their fuels. This was a revival stage for the Indian rocketry, which had died with the demise of Tipu Sultan who died in a battle with the British in 1799.

At this juncture, India was not alone working on indigenous rocket systems; there were other countries in addition to the US and the USSR, as Germany, France and Britain. The missiles and warheads turned deadlier with the passage of time. Innovation, well it was there, but it also meant increased peril for the mankind. However, safety resides in power; if you have power, you can hope to be safe; the war with China in 1962 had taught this vital lesson. The initial targets had been met, and it was the time to take it to newer heights. India was also concerned that this technology should be used to serve peaceful purposes and to solve real-life problems; they should not become mere tools to flex your muscle and threaten the world.

Wider Responsibilities

As Kalam worked with his mind and heart on the different projects being assigned to him, being busy all the time, yet willing to accept more responsibilities, he established a rapport with Prof. Sarabhai, who was a visionary in true sense of the word. He would visit different laboratories and review the progress of work with the entire team. His style of functioning impressed Kalam a great deal, this is the reason that we can find him mentioning his name whenever he speaks of technology and satellites. Prof. Sarabhai believed that the staff should be so persuaded that it takes up an assignment from the core of the heart. He once said to Kalam, "Look, my job is to make decisions; but it is equally important to see to it that these decisions are accepted by my team members." He did not believe in passing orders to be fulfilled by his subordinates. He believed that a subordinate member may not be willing enough to undertake a job that he is not convinced about, so it should be clear to him; the goal should make sense to him; and this is a trait of effective leadership.

This was the reason that the words of advice given by Prof. Sarabhai often became the missions of life for many. As different laboratories at different places were involved in different projects, he did not want them to be taken up one after another, rather he wanted them to be developed concurrently, in a multi-dimensional fashion. As Kalam rose in hierarchy, he got an opportunity to work closer with Prof. Sarabhai, and he had an opportunity to read his mind. He found that his mind was capable of thinking about different aspects of a problem at a different plan than most can even think of. We can illustrate his multi-dimensional working style in several works, let us tell you about this style so far as the development of payloads for sounding rockets is concerned. He did not want to complete a particular payload at one time and fit it into the rocket and then take up the next. Rather, he sat with the team of payload scientists to discuss the matter exhaustively into finest details, giving exact instructions. These teams of scientists worked in different organisations and at different locations. This was how the sounding rocket programme was being carried out in the whole of the country, mainly depending on mutual trust; and this was also a guarantee for its success.

Kalam was a born teacher, he possessed a great power of persuasion, which we can see in the lectures that he delivered at a later time. Perhaps realizing this trait of him, Prof. Sarabhai assigned him the task of providing interface support to payload scientists. So, Kalam was involved in establishing interaction with scientists from different laboratories like the TIFR, NPL (National Physical Laboratory), PRL (Physical Research Laboratory); in addition, he was required to interact with payload scientists from the US, the USSR, France, Germany, France and other countries. At this juncture, almost all physical laboratories in India were involved in the sounding rocket programme, each having its specific mission and its own specific payload to work on. These payloads were required to be integrated to the rocket structure so as to ensure that they functioned well, as well as were able to withstand the pressures of extreme flight conditions. Some of the different types of payloads included X-ray payloads to look at stars; radio frequency mass spectrometers payloads to analyse the gas composition of the upper atmosphere; sodium payloads to ascertain wind conditions including its direction and velocity; ionospheric payloads to explore different layers of the atmosphere; and the like.

Kalam liked to read books, they were like his eternal partners. Whenever he worked on a mission, he was wont to find out adequate motivation in different writers. He often read Khalil Gibran who at one place said, "Bread baked without love is a bitter bread that feeds but half a man's hunger." Kalam found these words very much applicable to his work. He realised that a hollow, half-hearted success can only breed bitterness. Giving extension to this advice from the great writer, Kalam says that if you didn't work with the mind and heart, your success would but be half, not doing justice to your clients. He says that one should choose a profession that he wants to choose. If a person wanted to become a lawyer or doctor, but happened to become a writer, his written words would feed but half the hunger of his readers; similarly, if a teacher, who wanted to be a businessman, would not be able to quench the thirst of learning in his students; nor would a scientist attain success if he did not want to be a scientist. If it is a mere chance, and not choice, that brings a person into a profession, he has two options before him: cultivate aptitude for it, or give it up.

The team work, capped by apt leadership by Prof. Sarabhai, led to the birth of two Indian rockets at Thumba. They were named Rohini and Menaka after the two mythological dancers in the court of Indra, the king of Gods. This was a great achievement as now the Indian payloads no more needed to be launched by French rockets. Prof. Sarabhai had played a key role in leading the team to this great accomplishment; he had created an atmosphere of trust and commitment at the INCOSPAR. Building upon his own knowledge and skills, he called upon each member to put in their best skills towards completion of the objective; he allowed each member to feel like a vital link in the chain, and extracted the best out of each.

Prof. Sarabhai knew at all moments how to lead his team, and accordingly, he used his skills of leadership in a variety of ways, which made each member committed towards the goal. He expressed disappointment when things went awry; but this was not to discourage his team members, he advised them suitably and guided them to the right course of action. At the same time, when things were not going in the desired direction, he would make things look more positive than they actually were. He used his power of persuasion to make his listeners spellbound. He used other techniques to motivate his members, as to bring in a technical collaboration from the developed world, thus giving his team members a subtle challenge to do their best as per their capabilities.

Kalam praises Prof. Sarabhai on several scores, but he liked how he dealt with failures. When massive projects are being taken up, even a minor slip can lead to the failure of the entire system, but does it mean that the entire project has failed? Prof. Sarabhai thought otherwise. He was always there to morally boost his team members when things did not go the way they were expected to. He would always appreciate the work put in and the things that were accomplished well, and would work to rectify shortcomings. Not only this, he also keenly observed if any of his team members had been assigned a task beyond his capability or skill; in that case, he would reassign the work such that his capability or skill can be utilised optimally and pressure on him could be lowered so as to bring out a better performance out of him.

Prof. Sarabhai had taken up a massive challenge, though he was understaffed and overworked; by the time the first Rohini-75 rocket was launched from the TERLS on 20 November, 1967, the entire team had acquired a very professional outlook. Kalam was in his heart embracing for a higher goal, that was destined to come his way sooner than later.

Kalam aptly advises that it is meaningless to be, 'a round peg in a square hole'; this can bring personal unhappiness and failure. A person having aptitude in a certain field is the most adequate worker, no less than him is the one who, finding himself in a profession by chance, cultivates suitable aptitude and does enough to do justice to the work. The missile project is so large that it involves several hundred scientists who work day in and day out; they all have to coordinate with one another so that the performance is achieved.

Indigenous VsImported

There are often suggestions that the foreign-made things are better than the indigenous ones. In fact, this suggestion comes from the sense of self-pity, out of indifference for the native wisdom. Kalam too faced this scenario on more than one occasion. Let us tell you about one.

Prof. Oda worked at the ISAS (Institute of Space and Aeronautical Sciences), in Japan as an X-ray payload scientist. He was completely dedicated to his work, putting his soul and heart into the work. He would bring X-ray payloads from the ISAS, which along with X-ray payloads developed by Prof. UR Rao would be engineered by Kalam's team to fit into the Rohini rocket. These X-ray payloads were required to be separated by an explosion of pyros triggered by an electronic timer, by which the X-ray payloads would be exposed to the space for collecting their data from the stars.

Kalam was at his work to integrate Prof. Oda's payloads with his indigenous timer devices. However, Prof. Oda did not seem convinced with the indigenous ones, and insisted that the Japanese timer might be used instead. Kalam felt that the Japanese timer was flimsy, and did not want to use it, but Prof. Oda stuck to his stand. Kalam yielded to his confidence. The rocket was launched excellently and attained the intended altitude. However, there was a hitch, the telemetry signal reported mission failure, which was on account of timer malfunction, leaving Prof. Oda in tears. He had worked hard, but this failure demoralised him somewhat.

RATO System

During one of his visits to Thumba, Prof. Sarabhai had advised Kalam to study RATO (rocket-assisted take-off) system. Kalam was trying to upgrade his knowledge about this system from all possible resources, but such that his work at Thumba was not disturbed. But now, the initial target had been met and the first Rohini-75 rocket had been launched, there could be avenues for a more important project for him. The intervening period was leisurely, in

The First Leap

which he tried to make up with the things he could not handle owing to his hectic schedule.

The year 1968 promised a better horizon of work for Kalam. It had not been many days into the new year when he was asked to see Prof. Sarabhai in New Delhi urgently. Filled with encouragement at this invitation, Kalam knew that something important was coming. Was it RATO? He thought but could not be sure.

Kalam reached Delhi and contacted Prof. Sarabhai's secretary for an appointment. He was asked to meet him at 3.30 a.m. at Hotel Ashoka. It was winter, to which he was little accustomed right since childhood, as he hailed from a region with a warm and humid climate. The untimely hour of 3 in the early morning was a bit uncomfortable, yet he knew how unusually Prof. Sarabhai worked.

Kalam finished his dinner and decided to wait in the hotel lounge. He did not want to sleep; he felt he might not be attentive enough, which he could not afford to be in the presence of a stalwart like Prof. Sarabhai. There were two things that Kalam liked to do during his free time. One was to think over spirituality and the other to read books. He was thoroughly a spiritual man, having a working partnership with God. In his heart, he always thought that he was not capable enough to undertake the vital projects that were being assigned to him, yet he promised to work hard and surrender everything to God. He always felt that nothing in the world could be accomplished with the divine blessing; and it was from this feeling that he derived strength, motivation and ideas. He said that the divine kingdom is within each one of us giving us strength and vitality, and it helps to achieve goals and realise dreams, but you have to surrender yourself to the divine manifestation.

The appointment was still far-off; it is all the more difficult to pass the time when you are doing nothing. Kalam looked around and found a book nearby. It was a book on business management, a subject in which Kalam was little interested. However, he picked it up and started to skim over paragraphs, reading a line here and there. He did not find it much interesting, and was about to close it, when he happened to see a quote from George Bernard Shaw, an Irish dramatist and socialist: "The reasonable man adapts himself to the world; the unreasonable one persists in trying to adapt the world to himself. Therefore, all progress depends on the unreasonable man." In no time, Kalam recalled another quote from the same dramatist: "Imagination is the beginning of creation. You imagine what you desire, you will what you imagine and at last you create what you will."

During the course of your imagination and working, a project is subjected to elements of uncertainty and ambiguity; these are not setbacks, rather they are the strengths, you deal with them to overcome all those failures that might have otherwise taken place. It was still 1 a.m., and the appointment was two hours away. Prof. Sarabhai was not a man to follow the beaten path; he was successful because he loved to flout the established rules and create new ones.

Kalam was sitting on the sofa for long, and he was not sure what to do at that odd hour. About this time, there was a visitor in the lounge; he sat on the sofa opposite Kalam's. Well-dressed, well-built person he was, with a blend of intelligence and alertness manifest on his face. Kalam wondered if he too had an appointment with someone at that unusual time. After a brief look at him, he sank his glance in the book, when he was intimated that Prof. Sarabhai was ready to receive him. As he rose, he noticed that the intimation to enter the same room was also given to the newcomer. He wondered if he had anything common with him.

Indeed, Prof. Sarabhai had called both of them together. The other man was Group Captain V.S. Narayanan from Air Headquarters. After the initial pleasantries, Prof. Sarabhai

The First Leap

set down to unfold his mission, it was none else but RATO, about which he had once asked Kalam to focus attention. Hot coffee was ordered to awaken the ideas that could have dimmed at that hour. It is vital for air force fighter and bomber aircraft to need a smaller run-up to become airborne, especially when they are operating in hilly areas where a long runway may not be available; also, during wars, the enemy might have destroyed part of the airstrip, disallowing the fighter aircraft to take off. There could be some other eventualities for use of this system, such as while carrying more than the prescribed load or during bouts of very high ambient temperatures. The RATO system could help the aircraft to take off from a short airstrip or runway with the help of a rocket-assisted boost. As substantial part of North India comprises hills and high mountains, this system could become very useful. The Indian Air Force needed this system to equip its S-22 and HF-24 aircraft. India had taken part in two wars in 1962 and 1965; and they brought to the surface a shortcomings that India was suffering with: indigenisation of military hardware and weapon systems. The RATO could help achieve part of this drive.

The ever energetic Sarabhai then asked the two to accompany him to Tilpat Range on the outskirts of Delhi. It took them about an hour. There he showed the two companions a Russian RATO and enquired of them if they could accomplish the task in eighteen months if he got them the motors from Russia.

The two companions, Kalam and Narayanan brimmed with confidence, and almost said in a chorus, "Yes, we can!"

The positive attitude helps to realise goals, and it was available in abundance. Prof. Sarabhai dropped them back at the Hotel Ashoka and then went to the Prime Minister's house for a breakfast meeting for a final decision. By the evening, the media was abuzz with the news of a new project, based on indigenous technological development, which could help to shorten take-offs of high performance

military aircraft, with Kalam at the helm of affairs. Kalam felt a new wave of energy flowing in his body as his mind braced with the idea of accomplishing the goal within the given timeframe. Trust had been reposed in him, and he had to do everything possible to accomplish the task. He felt happy, grateful, as he remembered a couplet from an anonymous poet, who meant:
> "Be ready for all days alike,
> Face them in due capacity,
> Bear when you are at the receiving end,
> And strike when opportunity calls."

Kalam, Narayanan and their teams set down to achieve this vital project. They studied the Russian systems and started work at the SSTC (Space Science and Technology Centre) in coordination with other agencies like the DRDO (Defence Research and Development Organisation), HAL, DTD&P (Air) and Air Headquarters. They introduced safety systems, such as the fibreglass casing, and other necessary features which could make the system worthy. It was a project which also gave them ideas about other missile systems and space satellites.

The bureaucratic system in India is very lethargic. It suffers from several lacunae which become stumbling blocks in the path of progress. It plays its game within the ambit of set rules, which are inelastic in nature and do not allow deviation from following them. Then there is a long hierarchy to obtain approval to several proposals, and often, the approval is obtained when the rationale behind the proposal is already obsolete. In many cases, accountability is to several persons and accounting procedures are very tardy. The government establishments tend to be conservative so far as following the rules and regulations are concerned, and the RATO project needed some radical style of functioning, to which the government would not easily accede.

The First Leap

Despite all these hurdles, Kalam and his team, comprising about twenty engineers, accomplished the goal to a reasonable limit before he was given a more important task. Before taking up the SLV project, he had conducted the first static test of the RATO in the twelfth month from the day of commencement of the project. In the next four months, he and his team succeeded to conduct 64 static tests. Later, Kalam was also involved when it was successfully tested on 8 October, 1972 at Bareilly Air Force Station (in Uttar Pradesh). The air force tested this marvellous gift on the fortieth Air Force Day. In it, a high performance Sukhoi-16 jet aircraft became airborne after a short run of 1200 m, as against a usual run of 2 km. The air force gratefully acknowledged the excellence of the system in the presence of Dr. BD Nag Chaudhary, then the Scientific Advisor to the Defence Minister. It not only boosted the performance of the fighter aircraft, it also helped to save vital foreign exchange. The native RATO could be produced at a cost of Rs. 17,000 apiece, and it replaced the imported RATO which cost Rs. 33,000. It also meant that the country no more needed to depend on the foreign suppliers for the vital equipment.

Kalam gave credit for this achievement to Prof. Sarabhai, though it was he himself who had worked on it heart and soul, and this brings to the fore a vital quality of a leader. This is an important quality of a leader to take responsibility for a mistake and give credit to the others for any accomplishment. This was what Kalam did.

□

7

The Missile Man

Self-reliance helps in more ways than one, this is the reason that boost to indigenous technology should be given. The imported systems have several shortcomings, such as supply of equipment and systems when they are needed the most. Since independence, India has faced this type of roadblocks on more occasions than one, and indigenization provides a vital answer to this problem. An accompanying problem with indigenous production is that the foreign partners do not will to share technology, so effort has to be made within the country to come out with newer forms of technology. The two wars in the 1960s and the imminent threat of yet another in the coming times stared in our eyes. Depending on foreign arsenals could not be a worthwhile proposition, so indigenous development was encouraged.

While Kalam worked on the RATO system, Prof. Sarabhai came out with a ten-year profile for space research in the country. It was intended to be transformed into a space research programme later. The main point of this profile was utilisation of satellites for different purposes, as for television broadcasts, meteorological observations and remote sensing for management of natural resources. The vital part of the profile was development and launch of the satellite launch vehicles, an ambitious project; it was a domain in which India was already making some headway, but it was negligible going by the standards achieved by developed countries.

This profile also aimed at easing out foreign cooperation, which was very prominent during the early years; more emphasis was being laid on self-reliance and indigenous technologies. The most important of these was the development of an SLV (Satellite Launch Vehicle) by which indigenous lightweight satellites could be injected into a low earth orbit. This programme had to be supplemented with several other systems like upgrading of Indian satellites from laboratory models to space entities and development of a wide range of spacecraft and their subsystems.

With these goals in mind, a Missile Panel was formed in the Ministry of Defence; both Kalam and Group Captain Narayanan were inducted in this panel. The groundwork in satellite and rocket had been done, and now was the time when the nation could think of developing its own missiles for defence purposes. The idea was to develop both strategic and tactical missiles. The distinction between these two types of missiles is fine. A strategic missile is mainly used to hit strategic targets within the enemy territory, rendering it incapable of functioning; while a tactical missile is mainly used for actual battle purposes to change the course of fighting. In that sense, a strategic missile has a longer range than a tactical one; but this distinction does not hold water, especially when the latter are deployed deep within own territory, as is done by America in the case of Tomahawk, which, despite a long range of 3,000 km, is used as a tactical missile.

At this time, India imported all its missile systems from Russia; the Defence R&D taking place in the country was heavily dependent on the imported equipment. Indigenous development required to first learn from the experiences of other countries and develop our own. Kalam and Narayanan sat together on more occasions than one to plan the project and acquire necessary equipment wherever they might be available, including Russia and other western countries.

Kalam worked with Prof. Vikram Sarabhai from 1963 to 1971. This was a great learning experience for him as he matured from a young engineer to a specialist in his field, rising from position-to-position. This was the reason that Kalam has sung ineffable eulogies for the Professor. In one stance, he likened him to a cow whose calf is tied to a peg while she roams around to graze, and she returns to the calf when her udders are full, to empty them in her little naughty child. Prof. Sarabhai went from place-to-place looking for ideas and assigned the fruitful ones to his team members to execute them to their logical conclusion. He had no dearth of new ideas and could suppose things well before they might happen; a true visionary he was. He exactly knew the capability of each component of his team.

It was owing to the vision of Prof. Sarabhai that the Indian scientific community could ever think of developing our own satellite launch vehicles to launch remote sensing satellites in sun-synchronous orbit and communication satellites in geo-synchronous orbit from the Indian soil. The design project of the SLV-3, India's first satellite launch vehicle was taken up at the VSSC (Vikram Sarabhai Space Centre). As the project involved multifarious and multidimensional efforts, different project leaders were selected to look after different systems. Kalam was given the design project of the fourth stage, that is, the upper stage rocket which was to be used to give the final velocity to put Rohini into orbit. Maybe he had been inducted for the job because of his specialisation in the field of fabrication technology, because the fourth stage called for a large number of innovations in this technology.

Kalam, along with his team, was working on the design when Prof. Sarabhai visited the facility with Prof. Hubert Curien, Chairman of CNES, the French space agency. During the presentation, Kalam realised a pleasant surprise that the fourth stage, being developed by him, was also being considered as upper stage for the French Diamont P-4 launch vehicle, though it required to double the size of the propellant as well as the entire size. So, an instant decision was taken in the same meeting to reconfigure the fourth stage to match with both Diamont P-4 and SLV-3. It was an exhilarating experience for Kalam because Prof. Sarabhai was completely confident about the Indian talent to finalise the project despite the Indian team still being at the design stage. The visitor from the French agency was so impressed by the well-planned and well-thought-out way of working that he did not hesitate to accept the project for the Diamont P-4.

A year later, when Prof. Curien revisited, he testified on review of the year's work that Kalam and his team had achieved in this period what their counterparts in Europe could not have managed in three years. He noticed that each component of the team worked up and down the hierarchy; calibre meant more important than rank or post. Kalam also believed in calling frequent meetings with all team members.

This new venture boosted Kalam's team and development started at a great pace. Unfortunately, in 1971, Prof. Sarabhai passed away. Another setback was also in store. The French government called off the Diamont P-4 programme too. It was a setback which Kalam tended to equate with the failures he had met, first at Dehradun when he could not be selected as an air force pilot, and second when the Nandi project was aborted at the ADE. The French venture had been called off when much work had already been done and it was near completion.

The death of Prof. Sarabhai was a more massive shock for Kalam. The two had interacted on numerous occasions, so they had built a rapport. The two minds with abundant positive energy always produced marvellous results. They discussed each point in detail, so that execution could become a reality. Just in context, we may like to inform that the wife of Prof. Sarabhai, Mrinalini Sarabhai, a classical dancer, has died recently on 21 January, 2016.

Kalam was required to attend the missile panel meetings, usually held in New Delhi. He attended one such meeting on 30 December, 1971, and as he was about to board an aeroplane for Trivandrum, he spoke to Prof. Sarabhai on telephone informing him about the salient points of the meeting. On this day, Prof. Sarabhai was on a visit to Thumba. He advised Kalam to wait for him at the Trivandrum airport itself for a meeting.

A few hours later, when Kalam landed at Trivandrum, he felt the atmosphere gloomy and his heart reeling under melancholy. He did not know why he felt so, because earlier, whenever he was scheduled to meet Prof. Sarabhai, he felt a flow of energy in himself. Soon he came to know why his heart was sinking into melancholy; Prof. Vikram Sarabhai had passed away a couple of hours ago following a cardiac arrest. Kalam greatly grieved at this tremendous loss. A harbinger of science was no more; a source of inspiration was extinct; the lamp of eternal energy was extinguished. The quality of leadership is manifested by the fact that of all 22 scientists and engineers that worked with Prof. Sarabhai went on to take up projects of national importance in the times to come, this was the way he had groomed talent. Indian science and technology would ever remain indebted to him. Kalam termed him as 'the Mahatma Gandhi of Indian Science', who generated leadership qualities in his team and inspired them through both ideas and example. Mistakes can delay or prevent the proper achievement of the objectives of individuals and organisations, but a visionary like Prof. Sarabhai can use errors as opportunities to promote innovation and development of new ideas.

To pay a tribute to the departed soul to whom it owed its existence, the entire complex at Thumba was integrated and renamed as VSSC (Vikram Sarabhai Space Centre). Earlier, this complex composed of the TERLS, SSTC (Space

Science and Technology Centre), RPP, RFF (Rocket Fabrication Facility) and PFC (Propellant Fuel Complex).

Despite these setbacks, the work on the project continued. Kalam completed the project ahead of the first three stages by at least five years. Despite the French call-off, it had been a very satisfying experience as he had worked hard and achieved success. Overcoming initial disappointment, he looked for other avenues where he could keep himself busy. The little vacuum created by this incident was soon filled up when his RATO was put into operation at Bareilly. We have told you about it earlier.

Mistakes are part of the game. In Kalam's words, "The price of perfection is prohibitive." Mistakes form part of the learning process, so he always preferred a dash of daring and persistence to perfection; he impressed upon his team members to pay vigilant attention to each of their attempts, because failures are stepping stones to success. He said to his colleagues, "Never mind being unsuccessful, what should be reinforced at every turn is 'improved learning'."

As the project assigned to Kalam was of national importance, he himself was under doubt if he was doing it in the right direction. He tried to be a valuable facilitator for his team members and provided them every kind of support they needed, yet he felt he had faltered somewhat, so he sought professional help. We have a lesson from this kind of working on his part, don't shy to seek help if you think it is needed. You may not accept the advice given to you, but it certainly puts you in a situation where you are able to oversee all the actions that you have taken until that time; it gives you the right perspective.

This project taught Kalam valuable lessons in leadership. Accept each component of your team as full partner in the scheme of things. He liked to share at each meeting everything, even the smallest achievement, that had been realised. The sense of commitment and teamwork is required to be rooted in trust, and he did it to perfection.

He also learnt the management aspect of leadership. You have to create leaders within your team who can take over the task at different stages.

Bertrand Russell said, "The trouble with the world is that the stupid are cocksure and the intelligent, full of doubt." After Prof. Vikram Sarabhai's demise, Prof. Satish Dhawan took over the VSSC as the director. The work on the SLV went on in full swing at the VSSC. Everything was being put in place right from design to development of procedures and technologies. There was a hitch being faced. The work for the SLV was being undertaken at a number of work centres spread over a large area as it was a mega project, and needed coordination of different agencies and departments, each of them functioning at their own rates and in their own ways, each having their own style of management. The SLV project was aimed at launching a 40-kg satellite into a 400-km circular orbit around the earth.

The lack of a management structure among all these agencies and departments caused a little difficulty, so Prof. Dhawan, in consultation with Dr. Brahm Prakash, picked Kalam for the job of coordination. He was appointed the Project Manager of the SLV. Kalam was doubtful of his capabilities to undertake this management job, as he was essentially an engineer; with his service, he had learnt some management, but taking it over at this scale could be disastrous. Moreover, there were more experienced men available to do the job. He articulated his doubts to Dr. Brahm Prakash. He smiled and said, "Don't focus your mind on other people's strengths compared to your own." He advised him to look at his capabilities and use them to expand the abilities of the people involved in the project.

Dr. Brahm Prakash went on to advise him on the kind of job he was expected to accomplish as the project director. He said that he had to oversee that each component worked to do its bit to the project. Kalam realised that his success on the project depended on the kind of work others did; so he had to be tactful, knowledgeable, tolerant and patient. He had to classify the workers on the project. Some people think the work more important, while for others, the workers are more important through whom the work can be accomplished. Then there are some who are interested in neither work nor workers, they are the work-shirkers, and it is necessary to deal with them in the right spirit, to make them realise the vitality of the work they were involved in and how they were involved in making history. He sat down to consider his options and decided that he would motivate his workers to do the work; this way he could ensure that work and workers proceeded together towards the desired direction. He visualised his team as a compact group in which each worker worked to enrich the entire team; he wanted each one of them to derive joy from the collective achievement at every stage of development.

The SLV project was large and needed a professional outlook to handle it. Kalam thought about it giving attention to every minute detail, and then translated the primary project objectives into some major tasks in conjunction with the policy decisions, management plan, budget and the powers delegated to him. After this, in consultation with specialist advice, he formed three groups to carry out a variety of project activities, including testing and execution. To aid him on the task, four advisory committees were formed to advise him on specialised areas, like rocket motors, control and guidance, electronics and the like. He was also assured of the guidance of outstanding scientists of that time.

"God helps those who help themselves," goes a popular adage. Kalam estimated that he needed about 275 engineers and scientists for the project to accomplish the goal within the given time frame of five years, but he could get only about 50. This was a difficult task as the project could be prolonged well beyond the time frame. But he came up with an idea. He decided to motivate his young engineers and scientists to undertake independent work on certain components of the project and put under them the required number of technicians, and synergised the entire effort. The young engineers and scientists, under the able guidance and supervision of the senior scientists, formed their own ground rules to do work efficiently as an independent team as well as inseparable part of the entire project. Whenever any of these teams tasted success, even a minor one, Kalam ensured that it was celebrated by the entire group, thus transforming it into a sort of mutual appreciation club. He allowed each team to work in the field of its specialisation with a great amount of freedom, which is very vital when you are doing some creative work. Kalam ensured that each team worked with self-motivation. This ensured a smooth functioning of the entire group, as well as development of the next generation of leadership to take up such projects in the future. Kalam, on his part, made his presence felt only as much as was adequately needed, no more, no less. He was always there to help any team member.

The massiveness of the SLV-3 project can be gauged from the fact that about 250 sub-assemblies and 44 major subsystems were conceived during the design stage, while the list of materials exceeded well over 1 million. When you need to manage a project at such an extent, you need to put in concerted and dedicated efforts, carefully looking to each system and subsystem, especially when the failure of a tiny part could well mean the failure of the entire project. A time of seven to ten years was conceived to arrive at a stage to achieve sustained viability of the complex programme. Prof. Dhawan promised to put all his resources and funds, including manpower at the VSSC and the SHAR, to the project. Everything could not be manufactured within the complex, so help was also needed from private and public industries, it needed interface with more than 300 industries for different parts and subsystems, while ensuring that each component did its job well enough, with a willingness to change the design, if need be. Acquisition of materials needed for the project was a very significant part of the project.

The project could be divided into three main parts: the mechanical structure, the electronics system to deal with the internal parts and the guiding systems, all of these aided by electrical circuitry. Fabrication of different parts needed metallic properties, ranging from stainless steel, aluminium, copper and others, in addition to making alloys which could withstand the purposes for which they were being made. In addition, non-metallic properties were needed which ranged over different types of materials right from ceramics, glass to fibre. Not only this, different materials had to be mixed in the right ratios to obtain composites, strong enough to withstand the pressures, duration and other needs of the project after it was put into orbit. Then there was also a lot of trial and error procedure, in which one material was tested first, and finding it inadequate, its substitute had to be selected. All these purposes required the specialist services of different types of engineers and scientists. In this process, to seek the contribution of private industries, they laid down detailed procedures; these procedures later became blueprints for many government-run science and technology business organisations.

When you are engaged with a massive work, of the scale of the SLV-3, time management becomes of utmost importance. Kalam realised this. He started his day with a long morning walk to get energy from the morning fresh air. Soon after, he was involved in multifarious work, which involved planning, attending meetings, overseeing teams, procuring materials, writing and replying to letters, undertaking reviews, giving briefings, and more. These tasks had urgent and conflicting demands on his time. To run all these errands smoothly, he planned his day during his morning walk.

Kalam loved to clean his office table himself. Having finished with this, he would first scan all the papers and files that were there waiting for his attention. He would give a few minutes to classify them into different categories. He will arrange them into a few piles of those that required immediate action, those that had low priority, those that needed to be read; he also classified them into those which needed just a fraction of time and which needed a sizeable time to finish. Mostly, he paid attention to those that required immediate attention, but at times, he liked to finish the work that required only a miniscule of his time, like signing letters drafted the previous day, or calling a department for collaboration work. This helped to reduce pending work greatly. When you are able to finish a few works within half-an-hour of coming to office, you feel invigorated and fresh, giving you energy to take up the other things.

Kalam set down on his task, dividing his priorities into three important parts: design capability, goal-setting and realisation of the goals from stage-to-stage. He also tried to provide a cushion to withstand any setbacks, which form an inevitable part of such a massive project.

An important part of the project was the information system, which needed a wide range of electronic system on the ground as well as in the vehicle, so that unimpeded contact with the satellite was maintained at all times. The signals received and sent had to be in intelligible ciphers, and it was to be perfectly ensured that this system worked well enough, because it would remain the only tool to track and keep the vehicle under control from the ground stations.

The most important part of all this was that the entire project was aimed at self-sufficiency and indigenous development and manufacture of all parts. The team members were confronted with a new project, and often they had none to seek guidance from. But they came together with the finest character, commitment and perseverance to bring out the most excellent design. During the course of their prolonged work, they faced problems regularly, but they kept working patiently. The working hours were often irregular, they needed to sit late at night, and often forgot about their lunches and dinners and families. Once Kalam wrote before rising from his table:

"*Again a deep silence engulfed the Universe,*
The cosmos seemed to be filled with energy,
The waves from both oceans went violently high,
And gently touched the feet of divinity
with beautiful shehnai playing with a divine song."

Despite his busy schedule and difficult position, Kalam maintained peace of mind, as these lines from him show. Not only this, he kept in touch with other aspects of science and technology he was earlier engaged with, like the RATO and the missile development. He was sad to know that the RATO was no more needed in view of the phasing out of the aircraft on which it was fitted and the new aircraft didn't need it. He was happy that the missile programme was proceeding at a fine pace at the DRDL, with Narayanan (now Air Commodore) at the helm.

Kalam was also appointed on a committee, in 1975, to evaluate the work so far accomplished at the DRDL. His inclusion was aimed at ensuring the smooth execution of aerodynamics, structure and propulsion of the missile. Kalam was satisfied to find that the missile team was doing a fine job, each of them worked with an intense desire to see an Indian missile take off, leaving no stone unturned in the process. It was very satisfying to see the adequate progress being made in that sphere, including hardware fabrication and system analysis. In some respects, the missile system was still in its infancy, yet it was proceeding at an adequate rate. The committee gave a strong recommendation to continue with the project, which was accepted by the government, and with this, the missile programme too picked up momentum, getting resources and manpower needed by it.

Step-by-step, the SLV work moved ahead and took a concrete shape. It was a slow but sure process. Individual teams were doing better, and now the stage was reached when their work had to be integrated, requiring Kalam to show his skills in supervision as well as direction. He encouraged the teams not only to attain their individual goals, but also to get in touch with each other so that their work could be in conjunction with each other. He allowed communication to flow from each direction, welcoming any ideas that could be received, even from the juniormost person.

During the course of the SLV project, there were, at times, anxious moments, especially when delays occurred owing to administrative and financial procedures; at one such meeting to discuss the delays, Kalam happened to lose his cool, which made even Dr. Brahm Prakash walk out. Kalam regretted for this unusual conduct; however, it resulted into a welcome outcome when Dr. Brahm Prakash delegated financial powers to the project itself, taking it beyond the powers of the financial and administrative personnel. This allowed Kalam the much-needed support and independence.

Personal independence for a professional can accrue from two things: knowledge and responsibility. Bacon rightly said that knowledge is power. Kalam said that this statement has to be upgraded: Up-to-date knowledge is power. If your power is obsolete, it does not stand a chance of gaining independence to work. With this in mind, Kalam advises that professionals should go back to basics, attend college and update their knowledge regularly. So far as personal responsibility is concerned, this can come from passion. When you take up a responsibility, you become all the more powerful, and you need passion. This helps you work for the things you believe in, resulting in true independence. The passion for work resulted into creation of several systems and subsystems, in connection with the

SLV-3, that were being done for the first time in the country. Independence helped to undertake work to which engineers had no prior exposure. Creation is a welcome step.

Kalam had many lessons to learn under the prudent and able leadership of Prof. Satish Dhawan, who looked into details minutely. He never hesitated to ask questions whenever he had any doubts, thus strengthening his learning at the same time. As it is, the path of the SLV involved revelation of several tenets of science, working with diverse people.

By the year 1974, several subsystems were reaching in their final stages, while work was still needed to be done in several others. Now, the target was to achieve the sounding rockets by 1975, sub-orbital flights by 1976 and the final orbital flight in 1978. As the volume of work to be done was still large, concerted efforts continued. There was a welcome statement on 24 July, 1974, when Prime Minister Indira Gandhi informed the Parliament, "The development and fabrication of relevant technologies, subsystems and hardware are progressing satisfactorily. A number of industries are engaged in the fabrication of components. The first orbital flight by India is scheduled to take place in 1978."

It was during Kalam's work on the SLV-3 that his childhood mentor, Jallaluddin died. It was a personal loss to himself and his family back home. His childhood memories came rushing into his mind, leaving him restless for several minutes. He remembered the activities that the two had taken together, right from building the boat to going round temples and walking on the seashore. He also remembered his soothing and motivating words when he had accompanied Kalam to admit him in the Schwartz High School or to see him off at the airport when he was scheduled to leave for the NASA. He made home to soothe his sister and nephew, who cried uncontrollably, but this was something that a person finds himself helpless about. His father was over one hundred years of age at this time.

Kalam has stated that he was never frightened of death, after all, everyone has to go one day; of course, for Jallaluddin, he went a little too early. He wanted to stay with his family longer, but he knew he could not, his calling was summoning him. Back at work, he still felt some hollowness within him for a few days. As he busied himself with the project once again, he found comfort in his work. He wrote:

"Silently merging many a day into night!
Making each part and testing my systems,
With care and delight of a creator's vision,
Hunger and sleep were submerged in mission!"

During the course of the project, Kalam suffered another blow in 1976 when his centenarian father too passed away. He had not been keeping well, especially after the death of Jallaluddin, and did not want to live more. Earlier, whenever Kalam learnt about his ill-health, he would take a city doctor with him, but his father would chide him for his unnecessary concern. "Your presence is enough to cure me," he used to say, but can a son be content to hear such words? He left this mortal world at the ripe age of 102 years, leaving behind fifteen grandchildren and one great-grandson.

With moist eyes, Kalam took leave of his mother to return to Thumba. His mother did not wish to stay away from the house of her husband, she said she was its custodian; and Kalam could not stay back, his destiny lay at Thumba. Unfortunately, she did not survive long after. At this time, he was scheduled to leave for France, where he had to resolve some knotty issues pertaining to the fourth stage, but he got the news; so he rushed to Rameswaram and performed the last rites. He wanted to stay at the place for a few days, but he could not. He had to return the very next day. But he wrote:

"I still remember a day when I was ten,
Sleeping in your lap,
To the envy of my elder brothers and sisters.

It was full-moon night, my world only you knew;
At midnight I awoke to tears on my cheeks
You knew the pain of your child, my mother.
Your caring hands, tenderly removing the pain,
Your love, your care, your faith gave me strength,
To face the world void of fear and with His strength
We will meet again on the great
Judgement Day, my mother!"

Kalam returned to his work, visited France and came back. About this time, von Braun visited Thumba. He was a German, who built rockets and later was captured in 1944 by the Allied Forces and then he was inducted into the NASA, building the Saturn rocket in the Apollo mission which put man on the Moon. When he saw the SLV-3, he praised it, but warned Kalam of the troubles that may lie ahead. He said, "...we don't just build on successes, we also build on failures." Hard work is not enough, you have to have a vision, he advised further. Hard work in mason-work can lead to giant structures, but a vision can transform the structure into a terrace with roses or a wall enclosing an apple garden. Commitment requires involvement, and that Kalam was doing his best despite three unfortunate deaths in the family in the short span of time. For him, total commitment is the common denominator among all successful men and women, and he wanted to get his name written among them. He thinks it immaterial how many hours you put in your work, each of the hour should be passed doing useful and meaningful things. When you do things with commitment, you derive from your work boundless energy; the more you work, still more you wish to work.

Failure and Success

The time had come on 10 August, 1979 to test whether the hard work undertaken over years had reached its perfection or not. It was the time for the first experimental flight trial of the SLV-3. At exactly 07:58 hours, the 23-metre-long, four-stage SLV rocket, weighing 17 tonnes, took off elegantly and immediately started to follow its programmed trajectory. The first stage went perfectly and it had a smooth transition to the second stage; it was like a dream come true, but it was shattered just a moment later. The second stage developed some problem, and it went out of control in no time. Just 317 seconds after lift-off, the vehicle plunged into the deep sea, 560 km off Sriharikota. It was a moment of profound disappointment. It was an unbearable loss to not only Kalam, but to all the scientists and engineers and other personnel engaged on the project. Once again, the fleeting memories of earlier failures passed from before his eyes. He had seen the unfulfilled success earlier, but this project seemed the most extreme despair. He found that his legs were unable to carry his weight, they could have sunken; he somehow controlled himself.

The questions were flying in the block house. Kalam wanted to find an answer, but it was no easy task to pinpoint a failure in such a massive project. The failure seemed unassailable, everybody wanted the answer, the nation wanted an answer, but he had none. He had hardly slept over the past week, and had been awake the whole of previous night. Completely tired, mentally and physically, he made to his room and slumped onto the bed. He was woken in the afternoon by none else but Dr. Brahm Prakash, who soothed his sentiments and invited him to lunch. The sad mind was provided some much-needed solace by him, when he said that it was no time to feel desperate, rather it was the time to rise and turn the failure into success.

Kalam recounted several failures that the scientists had faced before finally striking success; he felt confident in the company of Dr. Brahm Prakash, he regained his equilibrium when his companion said, "Big scientific projects are like mountains, which should be climbed with as little effort as possible and without urgency...you should climb the mountain in a state of equilibrium."

Another test came a little too soon, felt Kalam. It was planned for 18 July, 1980 in the morning hours. But the newspapers were all filled with all that can be described negative and discouraging. They recalled how the first test had miserably failed, drowning millions of rupees into the deep sea. He realised that the performance of the vehicle would determine the future of Indian space programme. Of course, not all newspapers were negative in their attitude, some hoped that the community of Indian scientists might have learnt a lesson from the previous failure.

At 08:03 hours, India's first Satellite Launch Vehicle, SLV 3 lifted off gracefully from the SHAR, and put the Rohini (the payload) into its low earth orbit. The success was achieved. Jubilation and celebration followed, while Kalam was carried on shoulders to facilitate him. The entive nation was excited as India was now among a small group of nations that possessed satellite launch capability. The event became the front page news. Greetings came from all quarters. What everybody celebrated was that it was a one hundred per cent indigenous effort.

Kalam had been facing failures, but this success eclipsed all his previous failures. But he felt alone when he wanted company, he wanted Prof. Sarabhai, his mother, his father and Jallaluddin to be with him in that hour of jubilation, but they had all departed from this material world.

Recognition

When you put in hard work, it is not certain if recognition will come necessarily. However, in case of Kalam, it came and rightly so, though there were people who felt that he was being singled out for the work in which a lot of people had actively and significantly contributed. He had to invest his time in delivering lectures, addressing the parliamentarians, receive commendation and the like.

Kalam was made the Director, Aerospace Dynamics and Design Group. The Republic Day next year brought recognition on a different plane: he was conferred with the Padma Bhushan.

Kalam could not think to rest in the glory that he had achieved. Now, he looked for other avenues where he could work and contribute in the national progress. The opportunity came to him the following year, in February 1982, when he was appointed the Director, DRDL. It was the same laboratory in which Narayanan had done substantial work on missiles. He finally joined the DRDL on 1 June, 1982. He found that the missile programme, run by Narayanan, had been shelved, and there was need to encourage the scientists and engineers there to contribute their best in the work.

Kalam decided that he could not allow the DRDL to work only in a single direction; he wanted to make the things which he could sell later, and did not want his scientists to live their lives making only one thing. He realized that the missile development is a multi-dimensional work, and work in only one dimension could not help it succeed. If you compared the ISRO with the DRDL, there was a shocking difference between the two, and this difference lay in the leadership. The former was lucky enough to have visionaries like Prof. Sarabhai and Prof. Dhawan at the helm; while the latter was not so lucky in this regard; in Kalam, supposedly it had found its first visionary leader.

Kalam said to his team-members, "You have to dream before your dreams can come true. Some people stride towards whatever it is that they want in life; others shuffle their feet and never get started because they do not know what they want, and do not know how to find it either."

Kalam encouraged and motivated his team and it culminated in the long-term GMDP (guided missile development programme). With this, plan was made to develop and manufacture a variety of missiles for both strategic and tactical uses, in addition to other scientific purposes. Kalam also wished to bring into practice his buried dream of a Re-entry Experiment Launch Vehicle (REX). Getting the government approval for the IGMDP (integrated guided missile development programme), instead of making missiles in phases, was like a wish materializing before it was asked. It was more than that Kalam and Dr. Arunachalam had dreamt, but the government was willing to commence the project; this could mean a new high for the country. It was a lesson for Kalam. If you have a success behind you, you can be sure to be taken seriously by others, and just this was happening. He was being given more than he had wanted.

India was going from strength-to-strength, and to develop a purely indigenous missile programme was thought to be very ambitious; but all involved people had to engage and devote themselves in the project to emerge with flying colours. After a prolonged discussion, it was planned to create a technology-oriented structure in the laboratory. A matrix type of structure was created in which different groups of scientists and technicians came together to work in the assorted tasks. The project started in all earnestness, with over 400 scientists and engineers working on the integrated missile programme.

With Kalam at the helm of affairs, he had to delegate his powers so that the entire project proceeded at a smooth phase; to start with, he examined his pool of talent and earmarked project directors, and appointed other personnel needed by them as per their task. While selecting important functionaries, he had to ensure that he chose the suitable people, and did not succumb to pressure, so he isolated himself from those down below the hierarchy, just to avoid any favouritism in the initial stage of the programme. He knew that selection of an unsuitable person as a project director or other important official could simply mean to jeopardise the entire programme, and he could not think of such a situation. During his search for the potentially right manpower, he observed his pool of talent, and came down to some very interesting conclusions. I think it would be useful to list them.

The working style of a person differs from that of another; it depends on how he plans and organises his tasks. He may be a cautious planner or a fast mover. The former carefully plans everything, while the latter goes about his job without a plan, action is the buzzword for him. Similarly, a person likes to concentrate all control in his hands, while another likes to freely delegate powers.

Kalam gave these characteristics a deep thought and decided that he wanted the people who treaded the middle path, and looked for the suitable people on these criteria. He looked for qualities like teamwork, welcoming ideas, respect for work and intelligence, and willingness to delegate. This was how the teams for the Prithvi, the Trishul, the Agni, the Akash and the Nag were formed. He ensured that both experience and new blood got place in his team. Everybody started to work in the right earnest.

When we speak of missile systems, especially aimed at indigenous development, a pertinent question arises in the mind. This is the country of Buddha and Mahatma Gandhi, the apostles of peace. Was development of missile systems contrary to their teachings? Moreover, no such demand for these systems had ever come from the armed forces until that time. There were several critics in the media. They said that India was still undeveloped and could not afford to invest its funds and resources for a mission that had a great element of uncertainty about it. One thing was, however, clear that if we wanted peace, we would have to be strong enough, as the Chinese aggression in 1962 had taught us adequately. If we go back into history, there was no question of Muslim conquest or the British conquest if the country was united and strong enough to bear with the onslaught. The missile system could prove a resource by which we could save a large amount of money and resources needed by the armed forces, and still emerge stronger. As the coming times would prove, the Indian scientists proved well enough that they could create world-class equipment with the minimum infrastructure and investment. India was set to enter a new era of technological development.

Disappointments and setbacks are an essential part of any development work; they were here too, but he made such arrangements by which his subordinates would not feel at a low ebb. He also created vistas through which their grievances, if any, could be redressed.

A question that often arose in the minds of people was: What was on his mind to prevent the entire programme going the way of the earlier shelved missile programme? Kalam had been wise; right from the planning stage, he had ensured that the programme comprised different stages until its justified end: that was, right from design stage to development stage to experiment stage to manufacture stage to deployment stage.

The existing space was insufficient to house all five missiles, so additional space was managed and the Research Centre Imarat (RCI) was made, which Kalam has described as the most satisfying experience. The test sites were also created, and the work on the missiles began in full scale. The first important step in the development of the missile system was taken on 26 June, 1984, when the shelved Devil missile system was revived, modifications were made to it, and launched with the newly developed computer system. This met all the requirements. This filled the scientists with confidence that they could do it, as more ambitious missile programmes were in the pipeline. So significant was its effect that all important people, including Prime Minister Indira Gandhi and media appreciated the effort. This type of appreciation boosted their morale like never before. The Prime Minister herself visited the DRDL and congratulated the entire team. How enthusiastic she was can be found out from the following dialogue that she had with Kalam. She asked, "When are you going to flight test Prithvi?"

"June 1987."

"Let me know what is needed to accelerate the flight schedule," she said with her bright eyes fixed at him, with a usual delicate smile on her face.

If you have this kind of leadership, you are sure to achieve results; the message was loud and clear, no impediment could be too big to hinder the project. Before she left, she added, "Your fast pace of work is the hope of the entire nation." However, she cautioned that no compromise should be made on excellence, and every effort should be made towards searching ways to improve upon the technology. Unfortunately, this doyen of political world was assassinated the same very year, but Kalam ensured that this did not make the missile programme suffer.

The sense of urgency was rooted in the very management system of the laboratory. In Kalam's own words, "...the work code in the Guided Missile Programme Office was: if you need to write a letter to a work centre, send a fax; if you need to send a telex or fax, telephone; and if the need arises for telephone discussions, visit the place personally." With this kind of ethics, the scientists at the DRDL, led by Kalam, did not disappoint the nation. Today, the IGDMP is known to be synonymous with excellence.

Kalam has always been very confident of the Indian talent. He quotes previous examples. He says when the green revolution was conceived, talent came forward, so did it come forward when the nuclear explosion was planned in 1974. And when the missile programme was underway, he could find coming into blossom new talent that could make the entire programme a reality, and this talent was working in numerous laboratories and workshops across the country. However, he rued one thing. When the country exploded the atom bomb, it became the sixth in the world to do so. When it launched the SLV-3, it became the fifth to do so.

When are we going to become the first in some technological feat?

India is resilient enough to absorb shocks; after the death of Srimati Indira Gandhi, her son Rajiv Gandhi was sworn in, who went on to win the Lok Sabha elections with a comfortable margin. By this time, the work on the RCI (Research Centre Imarat) had been completed. The next year, on 3 August, 1985, the new Prime Minister inaugurated the new facility. He was very enthusiastic of the scientific work in general, and missile system development in particular. He promised the community of scientists that the nation would do everything to ensure to make their lives comfortable, so that the talent did not flow out of the national boundaries, especially at a crucial juncture when it was needed for technological innovation in the country.

A special note was also made to induct new talent in diverse activities of the DRDL, which now also required to develop a re-entry technology and structure, a millimetric wave radar, a phased array radar, rocket systems and other such equipment. The young scientists were, at first, unsure of the significance of the work they were assigned with, and once they were convinced, they set down to work. Sometimes, they looked for the senior scientists to work for. They were convinced that the real joy of something lies in the process, in doing it; when you have finished it, the joy becomes transient as you have to look for the next target. The young scientists were also involved in such activities as presenting their work in review meetings, this allowed them have an idea of the entire system. "You have to fear nothing; if there are doubts, we will work together to resolve them," Kalam said to them. The young scientists knew that the 'big shots', were with them, so they worked zealously.

The primary testing of the Trishul came early enough, on 16 September, 1985, it was launched from the test range at Sriharikota. The missile did well to meet almost all targets, with a small portion needing improvement. The subsystems too worked well, giving the DRDL further confidence that they were on the right path. The test flights were not to become the norm. The next in line was the launch of the Pilotless Target Aircraft (PTA).

All this while, Kalam also made effort to invite expertise from the academia. This was to ensure that the continuous inflow of talent continued. For this, he contacted several educational institutions, including the IISc, Jadavpur University, IITs and others. In their own institutions, they did significant work on subsystems of the missiles; for example, Prof. I.G. Sharma developed the air defence software for multi-target acquisition by the *Akash*. The challenges were numerous as the missiles needed a large number of subsystems, but they were adequately planned.

In any organisation, especially in the government departments, a job is considered very uncharitable, and time for it comes every year, this is the time to fill the annual confidential reports (ACRs) of the subordinate staff. The problem with this process remains that the Boss cannot mark all of his subordinates 'excellent' even if they are working at their top capability; and when he happens to mark a person not so favourably, it is taken as a personal dislike. Kalam too had faced this dilemma. So, this is the time when subordinates try to please the Boss rather than do actual work they are assigned with. The problem becomes all the more acute because ACRs are closely linked with promotions and postings. Thus, the Boss has to deal with hopes on one side and apprehension on the other. Kalam tried to be a fair judge, though it remained a critical proposition. He looked for inner motivation in people, and not mere intentions.

With the commencement of 1988, the preparation for the launch of the Prithvi missile started to be made. It was finally launched on 25 February the same year from Sriharikota. It was a history in creation, because what shocked the unfriendly and western countries was not the firing of the missile, but its accuracy. It had an accuracy of

50 metres CEP (circular error probable); that means that it could strike within 50 m radius of the target. The western countries were, in particular, angry and they clamped a technology embargo on the country, making it impossible for us to buy anything even remotely connected with the development of guided missiles. India knew that it was coming, so all focus was kept on indigenous development right since the beginning. Their embargo only further firmed up the will to achieve the next targets.

The next in line was the Agni. Involvement, participation and commitment were the ethos at work in absolute terms. Everybody in the team worked to perfection, giving slip to personal comforts. When the date for the launch was fixed on 20 April, 1989, there was great international pressure to hold back the trial, in fact advocating to suspend the entire development of the project. However, the Government of India stood behind the DRDL like a rock. The media too circulated reports that the political leadership was under a great international pressure and could succumb to it. And as things went, some problems occurred during the countdown, owing to which the launch had to be postponed. It is easy to criticise. There were opinions in the air that the launch had been aborted owing to the pressure, but it was not the fact, as the later experience would show. When the launch was rescheduled for 1 May, 1989, and had to be postponed again, the media went berserk. For one newspaper, the term IDBM stood for Intermittently Delayed Ballistic Missile.

But Kalam and his teams knew the fact and were confident of overcoming the shortcomings. Moreover, the things had not been as bad as had been with the first launch of the SLV-3, which had plunged in the deep sea; their missile was well with them. Kalam gathered his companions and said, "The country deserves no less than success from us. We have to do it and do it to perfection."

The next launch of the Agni was scheduled for 22 May, 1989. As the countdown began, anxiety could be noticed in the scientific fraternity involved in the project, while the critics tried to pick any shortcomings if they could find. Mr. K.C. Pant was the Defence Minister then. He was there at the launch site. After two postponements, in fact, three because the third scheduled date was not announced, curiosity had been replaced with eagerness. Will the launch be successful? This question eclipsed every mind. Pant felt this, so he asked Kalam, "What would you like me to do to celebrate the successful launch of the Agni?"

The media pressure had told upon Kalam, so he did not find an answer for some time, and then he controlled himself, coming to terms with the prevailing situation, and said, "I would like 1,00,000 saplings planted at the RCI."

"Then you need not worry," said Pant emphatically and in an upward mood, "You have sought the blessings of the Mother Earth, you will have success tomorrow."

The forecast came true. The next day, the Agni took to the infinite sky-like it had practised several times before; it was like a swan that takes to its wings in an effortless manner. Overcoming the adverse media, negative international pressure, technical snags and eagerness, the launch was as successful as successful can be. It was an era of ordeal, that had been overcome. The eager faces turned jubilant, the media sang eulogies in praise, forgetting their adverse comments; any way, this is the way the media functions. Celebration followed. The President and the Prime Minister showered praise on the scientists. The people felt themselves stronger, while the unfriendly nations felt pangs of envy.

As it happens, there were speculations that the effort was not completely indigenous; some papers in the world carried articles that technology for certain stages and subsystems was sourced from western countries, like Germany and France. Kalam could only laugh at them. He

only remembered the famous lines from Jallaluddin Rumi, a philosopher:
> "Be a lamp, a life boat and a ladder.
> Help someone's soul heal.
> Walk out of your house like a shepherd."

What was the Agni going to do to our military strength? Our armed forces were built to undertake defensive operations, barring some small scale offensive roles, as we lacked deep penetration equipment. With the successful launch of the two missiles until then, the Indian armed forces were infused with strength to undertake even deep penetration, they could strike well within the enemy territory, and with precision. The work on the Nag and the Akash continued; these could put India into a position of strength in the world community. The confident nation also looked forward to the development of other systems, like the LCA (light combat aircraft), air-to-air missile Astra, third generation anti-tank missile system with 'fire and forget' capability, and other systems. The subsequent launches of the Prithvi and the Agni too proved successful, which also materialised into raising their capability as well as range. The capability stared in the eyes of any state-of-the-art technology in the world.

The nation celebrated the success of its missile programme in 1990, when Kalam and two of his colleagues: Dr. Arunachalam, J.C. Bhattacharya and R.N. Agarwal were conferred with the Padma awards. Kalam had got the Padma Bhushan after the successful launch of the SLV-3, it was now the highest Padma award: Padma Vibhushan that was conferred on him. As a sense of contentment dawned on Kalam when this news broke, he thought if anything could be greater than this recognition from the countrymen. He spared a thought for those scientists, engineers and other professionals who left the Indian shores to earn handsome monetary awards abroad, but can they ever hope to attain this type of contentment and appreciation from the countrymen. Love and respect cannot be measured in monetary terms, he concluded.

In 1990, Kalam was conferred with the honorary degree of Doctor of Science by the Jadavpur University at a special convocation. What made this occasion special was the fact that the legendary Nelson Mandela too was conferred with this honour with him. Kalam wondered if he was eligible to be honoured at par with this great leader. Perhaps their sense of total commitment brought them at par; they shared the same passion for their respective fields, one in bringing happiness to masses, and the other in developing indigenous technology for the country's development.

The launches culminated into user-trials; there is no sense in acquiring technological capability if it is not to be used in practice.

In 1991, the Gulf War began, and the live war was brought into people's drawing rooms through television satellites. As people were glued to their television sets, a pertinent question naturally rose in their minds, if our Prithvi and Agni and Trishul could match up with the Scuds and Patriots. There was a ray of optimism when Kalam responded with an emphatic 'Yes'. The country could rest in security after the massive work undertaken by the scientists. This war also brought forth the fact that the future wars belonged to missiles and electronic warfare, instead of infantries and armoured columns infiltrating into the enemy territory: the very concept of fighting was set to undergo a sea change. The Gulf War showed in abundant measure that the future wars could be won only on the strength of technology. In fact, the history of military conflicts have proved this fact right since the beginning of battles. Babur had been able to defeat Abdali on the basis of his cannons. India's problems worsened when our rulers did not pay adequate attention to technology or did not keep up with it. Tipu Sultan is a fine example to quote. His missile technology excelled that of the British at the first war, but by the time the third and final war took place, his forces stood nowhere in comparison with technological excellence of the British, and the result was there for all to see. India had seen Pakistan induct super technological equipment like Patton tanks and Sabre jets by Pakistan; their dangers could be warded off only by the man behind the machine; but this could not be expected to yield desirable results every time the two countries clashed, so defence preparedness had to be rooted in strong technological fundamentals.

These issues came for discussion when efforts were started for further technological innovation so far as missiles were concerned. Now, attention was paid to their feasibility on the ground in a battle scenario, making every effort at reducing the CEP. The results were encouraging. Kalam had helped India achieve a position which was full of promises. India is a renowned missile power with its numerous projects in satellites, including Chandrayaan and Mangalyaan. With tremendous vitality, India is in an unassailable position where no country can afford to overlook us.

Kalam was inclined to recall a poem by Mautrana, a Chilean biologist, so far as his contribution in the missile programme was concerned. A portion of the poem reads thus:

> *"Show me so that I can stand*
> *On your shoulders,*
> *Reveal yourself so that I can be*
> *Something different."*

> *"Don't impose on me what you know,*
> *I want to explore the unknown*
> *And be the source of my own discoveries.*
> *Let the known be my liberation, not my slavery."*

❑

8
The Next Phase

As 15 October, 1991, the sixtieth birthday of Dr. Kalam, approached, he looked forward to retirement from the long government service, replete with a lot of feats. Though the missile programme still continued, he was confident that the new generations of scientists and engineers were capable enough to carry on the work efficiently. He intended to enter the field which he loved most but had not had time to undertake it; it was teaching. In particular, he wanted to devote himself to teaching underprivileged children. He remembered the words of Sarvapalli Radhakrishnan, India's second President and teacher-philosopher, "Teachers should be the best minds in the country." Kalam never thought that he possessed the best mind, but nevertheless he wanted to share his wisdom so that the legacy of science and technology could go on even after him. He wanted to inculcate the virtues of exploration and self-confidence in the youth, who were the future of the country. He wanted to make sure that the future of the country was safe in the young hands. He wrote sentimentally:

"I am a well in this great land
Looking at its millions of boys and girls
To draw from me
The inexhaustible divinity
And spread His grace everywhere
As does the water drawn from a well."

His friend, Prof. P. Rama Rao too was heading towards retirement shortly, and as the two discussed their retirement plans, both of them concurred to open a school; they even named it as Rao-Kalam School. Scientific excellence and technological innovation had been part of their lives, but they now wanted to look at other aspects of life which they had missed during their long stint with science and technology. However, not always things go the way you like. Man proposes and God disposes. They had to shelve their plan about the school, as the Government of India did not relieve either of them.

Until the government could form its idea about him, Kalam decided to write his memoirs, which was published in the form of the *Wings of Fire*, an autobiography. This book puts in graphic details about different aspects of his professional life as well as how he happened to reach it. The way he has dealt with his sentiments goes to show the depth of wisdom in him. He was a true human, true nationalist, true patriot and true scientist, all rolled into one.

In July 1992, Dr. Kalam was appointed as the Scientific Advisor to the Defence Minister and Director general of the DRDO, succeeding Dr. V.S. Arunachalam. At this time, P.V. Narsimha Rao was the Prime Minister and Sharad Pawar the Defence Minister. Kalam handed over the charge of the DRDL to Lt Gen V.J. Sundaram. By this time, the DRDL had transformed the Prithvi and the Agni from development to limited series production, aimed at meeting the field requirements of the user (the army) in terms of deployment and operation. Kalam bade farewell to the distinguished organisation that he had been part of during his illustrious career.

Nuclear Tests

Now known as the Missile Man, Dr. Kalam had to work for the national welfare in his new capacity. India was embracing itself for a new threat, that was from terrorists.

The expanding needs of the country to thwart terrorists' strikes proved a drain on the country's economy, it remains so even today. Prime Minister Narsimha Rao had initiated free market economy, yet much was needed to be done as the national economy was still weak. Moreover, with the disintegration of the USSR, India lacked the backing of any super power, and it was still miles away from attaining the status of a self-reliant power, let alone super power. Nuclear weapons afforded a viable option for the country, but could the country withstand the economic sanctions that could come with it?

Despite all these adverse conditions, Prime Minister Rao favoured to carry out nuclear tests. Preparations started secretly, in which Dr. Kalam had a role to play. Earlier in 1974, India had exploded atom bomb, but now India needed to carry out the test explosion again to infuse vital inputs in the system. The work went on discreetly, and the explosion was imminent in 1995. However, the United States got wind of the likelihood; it warned of the consequences; Narsimha Rao weighed his options keeping the economic sanctions in mind. He succumbed to the extreme pressure mounted on him by the international community. Despite abandonment of the nuclear explosion, no one could deny the capability that the country possessed.

After this, the country witnessed a little political instability. In general elections in 1996, the BJP (Bharatiya Janata Party), emerged as the largest party with a hung Parliament. Atal Behari Vajpayee was invited by President Shankar Dayal Sharma to form the government, but he could not muster support of half of the house, and resigned. The next to become the Prime Minister was H.D. Deve Gowda, but he did not want to get embroiled in the nuclear issue, so he allowed it to cool off.

After him to come to power was Prime Minister I.K. Gujral who was of the opinion that the time was not yet ripe for conducting the nuclear tests. However, he was a great admirer of Dr. Kalam and his scientific capability. His Defence Minister, Mulayam Singh Yadav too believed in the scientific prowess of this great scientist. Both of them believed that the nuclear tests could not be undertaken right then, but the man deserved the award of the Bharat Ratna, the highest civilian award in the country. The announcement to this effect was made in November 1997, and with this, Dr. Kalam became the second scientist, after C.V. Raman, to receive this coveted award. It was a befitting tribute to the great man for his scientific acumen and his contribution to India's missile and space programme.

However, the urgency to test a nuclear bomb was felt once again in 1998 when Pakistan tested its nuclear-capable Ghauri missile. Named after the dreaded invader, Ghauri Mohammad, it led to formation of a public opinion that a suitable response was needed to be given; however, political establishment lacked the will. This missile could strike in India's heartland, so there was need to equip the Agni with nuclear warheads, for which the tests were needed.

The same year, in the general elections, the BJP clearly advocated for the nuclear test, and received a mandate. With Atal Behari Vajpayee at the helm once again, the western world spied on India for any nuclear designs; the satellites started to watch any 'untoward' movement in India which could suggest a nuclear test. In the country, there was a consensus that India should become a full-fledged open nuclear power, unlike Pakistan which had developed its nuclear bomb clandestinely and was in the denial mode.

This time, the political will was right there, but the entire operation needed to be conducted very secretly as the bitter experience in 1995 had shown, when the U.S. had mounted unprecedented pressure on the Indian establishment, and consequently the tests could not be conducted. Clear instructions were issued by the Prime Minister that every care had to be taken to keep the move secret. He did not divulge any information even to his cabinet colleagues, including the Defence Minister.

Vajpayee did not lose much time and within a fortnight of taking over the power, he summoned Dr. Kalam and Dr. R. Chidambaram and authorised them to conduct the nuclear tests. Brijesh Mishra, the principal secretary to the Prime Minister, was to act as the sole liaison officer for the entire operation. As much of the work had already been completed previously and the test site had been kept ready ever since 1995, a month's time was thought to be enough. Whatever work was done there was undertaken in the dark of the night by the army. The 58 Engineer Regiment was entrusted with the job of constructing facilities.

In an attempt to maintain total secrecy, all civilian scientists and engineers were given code names and were all required to don army fatigues. In this effort, Dr. Kalam became Maj Gen Prithviraj, while Dr. Chidambaram became Maj Gen Natraj. Even the wells and shafts were codenamed, as Taj Mahal, White House and so on. It would not be prudent to divulge many details here. A sub-kiloton device was placed in the shaft. It was of low intensity because it was intended to be used as a tactical weapon; also vital scientific data had to be gathered so that adequate missiles could be produced using it. The explosion was not entirely meant for military purposes, it was also meant for peaceful purposes as the quantum of energy to be released from it had to be ascertained.

It was 11 May, 1998. India was ready to jump into its next status. Dr. Kalam and his team members were ready with everything. The only hitch was the wind which was blowing towards the Pokharan town, and they waited for it to die down. As they waited for the moment which was worth waiting for, anxiety was manifest on the faces. The Prime Minister was in his chamber with a secure hotline from the test site. At 3.00 p.m., Dr. Kalam called and informed that the wind had slowed down to the acceptable

The Next Phase

level and the test could be conducted in the next hour. The go-ahead was given. Just in three quarters' time, the first three devices were detonated simultaneously. The impact of the explosion was as much as to raise an area of about the size of a football ground to a few metres above the earth. Clouds of dust rose. The test was successful and met all the criteria. The government was quick to assert that now India had a proven capability for a weaponised nuclear programme.

Two days later, two more tests were conducted. In fact, three were planned for this day, but only two were conducted. As all the required criteria had been met in the five blasts, so the sixth device was saved. With this, India entered the select group of nuclear powers in the world, that possessed a lighter, more powerful weapon system, and it was no more clandestine. India had acquired creditable deterrence capability with it. The entire operation had been undertaken so secretly that the satellites watching over Pokharan were befooled into believing that normal military exercise was taking place there. It shocked the world, especially the western world, and a lot of international criticism came.

This test had yet another positive aspect. Until this time, Pakistan had been developing its nuclear bomb clandestinely, and did not accept that it possessed this capability. Within a fortnight, on 28 May the same year to be precise, it conducted the nuclear tests. Nuclear tests cannot be conducted at such a short notice unless due preparations were in place. With this, India had succeeded to bring forth the real face of the Pakistani establishment.

Nuclear weapons are mainly strategic in nature. When approached, Dr. Kalam emphatically asked why it was okay for Britain or America or Russia to possess them and not India. The western powers are not even ready to reduce the number of their nuclear warheads and they want India not to possess even a single warhead. Moreover, there was no way out for India but to have them when there were two inimical countries on its borders, both possessing nuclear weapons.

Years later, when Dr. Kalam was delivering a series of lectures at the Anna University, he was asked, during the interaction phase, that Amartya Sen, the great economist, had described India's nuclear weapon test ill-conceived, and if his views should be respected. Dr. Kalam said, "This is right that India should have friendly relations with all countries of the world in order to prosper economically, but can it sit back and overlook the threat from other countries? Pakistan, that stands nowhere in terms of economic development, ran a clandestine nuclear programme, not only this, it kept warning and threatening India with dire consequences, is it not appropriate for India to take defensive measures? Dr. Amartya Sen looks at India from the western perspective; he does not speak against the U.S. and Russia that have more than 10,000 warheads in their arsenals and do little to reduce them. Why do you want to deprive India of this shield?"

Dr. Kalam felt that he further needed to elaborate the answer, so he went on to add, "India has been subjected to invasions in the past 3,000 years, with a motive to occupy territory or spread their religion or drain the country of its wealth. Why is it that India never invaded other countries, with a few exceptions in the Tamil kingdoms? Are we not brave enough? No, we are brave, but we are tolerant too and never understood the implications of being ruled by others. Were the Indian rulers strong enough, would Britain have drained India of its natural wealth? Strength respects strength and not weakness. Military might and economic prosperity go hand in hand. You can have economic prosperity only when you are secure from external threats and invasions."

India was one of the founding members of the UN, yet it did not get a permanent seat in the Security Council. And today, when India has emerged as a militarily and economically powerful nation, there are countries that recommend it to be included in the expanded Security Council. It simply means that you have to have might to gain international respect.

Hidden Sacrifice

In nuclear test was also hidden a great sacrifice by the man we know as the Missile Man. When in 1998, Vajpayee returned as the Prime Minister, he telephoned Dr. Kalam about midnight and proposed that he wanted to induct him as the cabinet minister. This proposal had come suddenly, so naturally, Dr. Kalam required a little time to think over, so the appointment to see the PM was fixed at 9 a.m. next morning. Dr. Kalam was not able to decide what he should do about this important proposal, but at this time, he was handling two projects which were of national importance. He gathered a few of his well-wisher friends and sought their advice. The next morning, Dr. Kalam said to the Prime Minister, "Sir, I am now busy with two important projects; one is the Agni, we have to ready it for deployment; and the other is to embrace for the imminent nuclear programme. I suppose the time is right to devote myself to these projects, rather than get deviated from this orbit." A sleek smile appeared on the noble face of Vajpayee. He appreciated his feelings and allowed him to continue.

Work went on to build nuclear capability, as we have already told you, and on 11 April, 1999, the Agni-II was first tested with a full nuclear capability. It met its mission goals when it landed in the Bay of Bengal, 2,100 km away. Dr. Kalam was pleased at this success, and it was on such occasions that his inner poet came out with an eloquent expression. He wrote a poem in Tamil, we give you its English version:

"Far away in the Bay of Bengal,
Where the sea is deep and waves are high,

Agni lands with glory and light,
Awakening the nation with acquired strength."

As the world in awe praised doyens of deed,
Landed Agni, now surrounded by sea creatures,
Curiously asking the source of its origin:
'Who made you, Agni, and who shaped you, Agni?'

'Who all were behind this scintilluting feat?'
Pondered Agni, gasping for a while,
And delving into the past decided to speak:
'Scientists and engineers sweated it out.'

'Silently merging many a day into night!
Making each part and testing my systems,
With care and delight of a creator's vision,
Hunger and sleep were submerged in mission!'

'With enthusiasm and dedication in action,
Melted their desires in making me alive.'
'So well the scientists made you in such fashion,'
Sea creatures quipped in conversation.

Agni replied: 'No, not alone my friends,
Though motivation and desire are components of success,
Woven in heady mix of hard work and technology;
Yet, wives and mothers of my creators also.'

'Never allowed any problem to pierce my makers' hopes
And prayed in silence for success with lighted lamps
And they lighted the lamps everyday to keep up the hopes,
Hopes of millions merged with blessings of these women.'

'Beloved's love and affection of offspring,
Blessings of elders and glow of lamps lit by creators' wives;

*I came out of the light that was quite bright
With hope, vision and love.'*

*'When men and women are together,
Love and understanding are created,
Lamp of hope and creativity blossoms
And Agni with purity and strength emerges.'*

*'Nation grows, pride and prosperity bloom.'
Agni looked around, took a deep breath
And announced to those who were there all around,
'I emerged from the lamps lit by the mothers and wives of my creators.'*

Dr. Kalam worked with justice in mind. He firmly believed that national good was of paramount importance and the personal ego came the last. When in 1996, Pakistan acquired the Harpoon missile from the U.S. and the Exocet missile from France, the Indian navy was under a great threat, because it did not possess a missile system to counter these new threats, so it approached Dr. Kalam for a rescue and urgent action.

The Trishul missile was near Dr. Kalam's heart, he would like to see it being deployed as soon as possible, but its deployment had been delayed owing to a number of factors, and until then, the threat from Pakistan could not be overlooked as our naval ships had become susceptible, so he did not take much time to finalise the Barak missile system from Israel.

Dr. Kalam had also seen the success of the cruise missile during the Gulf War; it was incredible to note that a few hundred cruise missiles had destroyed the entire command and communication centres in Iraq in a short time and changed the very face of the conflict, bringing Iraq to its knees. Therefore, he favoured a joint venture with Russia, aimed at the design, development, manufacture and marketing of the supersonic cruise missile, that came to be known as BrahMos. The joint venture was the brainchild of Dr. Kalam, which helped Russia and India come together and share technology, while the strategic needs of the nation were being fulfilled.

The BrahMos was conceived to be innovated too. Dr. Kalam wanted it to be speedier enough, so he wanted it to be propelled at a supersonic speed in place of it being a subsonic weapon, like the Tomahawk. The credit for making BrahMos the fastest cruise missile in operation goes to none else but Dr. Kalam.

☐

9
Retirement is Still Away

In 1999, Dr. Kalam was looking forward to a retirement life, he wanted to realize his dream of being a teacher, but the government was in no mood to relieve him. To accommodate him in the government, the office of the Principal Scientific Adviser (PSA) was created and he was the first person to occupy this. There are few instances of such type so far as the Government of India is concerned, and brings out the importance that was attached to this great man. The government needed his services in evolving policies, strategies and support-systems needed in the field of science and technology to meet the diverse needs of national development and industry with a view to achieve economic prosperity.

As it was the new office, the charter of its duty was quite vague in the beginning, so Dr. Kalam himself set out to look for work, and it was in this process that he chose to undertake some social projects by which he could make the life of every Indian better. He focussed his attention on how to make life-saving medical treatments affordable to the Indian masses. For this purpose, within six months of his assuming office, he called a conference of about fifty medical experts, directors of government laboratories, researchers and industrialists in the Vigyan Bhavan. In it, a consensus was reached that lowering of costs of medicines and medical equipment was absolutely necessary to make them affordable to common people. They also found that in several cases, the actual costs were lower than the patients were being made to pay. It was also sure that the colossal multinational companies would not work for the welfare of the poor, so the Indian companies must step forward to bring out viable solutions for their own people. This conference resulted into three significant developments in healthcare field in India; these were: malaria vaccine, indigenous liver transplant and stem cell research on ophthalmology.

Dr. Kalam also took interest in agricultural development and initiated steps by which the farmers would be encouraged to adopt technology for their farming processes.

During his tenure as the Principal Scientific Adviser, Dr. Kalam was always looking for fields in which he could help people from different walks of life. For this purpose, he visited different organisations and departments, and met common people to further augment his knowledge about different aspects. When he visited Assam to be conferred with the honorary doctoral degree at Tezpur University, he questioned if the flood waters of the devastating Brahmaputra could be diverted to the other areas in need of water, like drought-hit Rajasthan.

Dr. Kalam was always looking for avenues in which he could apply his knowledge of science and technology to better the lives of people. However, he felt bitter when different states claimed their exclusive rights over the natural resources in the state to the exclusion of all others. He opined that the national interest must come first, always and every time. He made interlinking of rivers a mission for himself and tried to pursue it at various fora. He continued to pursue this subject after he became the President. He realised that only planned and better water management could meet the challenge of massive need of water in the country.

Dr. Kalam worked on the PURA (Providing Urban Facilities in Rural Areas) very vigorously during his tenure as the PSA. This idea was the brainchild of Prof. P.V.

Retirement is Still Away

Indiresan, the former director of IIT Madras. Dr. Kalam recalled his meeting with this great scientist, "When my friend Prof. Indiresan came up with the idea of PURA, it struck a chord." We shall discuss this topic in a little detail elsewhere.

On 30 September, 2001, during his visit to Bokaro in Jharkhand, Dr. Kalam survived a helicopter crash. He was on the verge of seventy years, and his plan for retirement was still eating dust. He had been using his free time to interact with students, but he wanted to do it on a larger scale. After this incident, he approached Prime Minister Vajpayee and requested him to relieve him from the government service. With the usual shiny eyes, he said, "Sir, do I deserve a leave after seventy orbits round the sun?" Vajpayee knew the worth of the man; he offered him a berth in the ministry, but Dr. Kalam politely declined the offer. The Prime Minister had no way out but to concur with his request.

The high point of his tenure as the PSA was the finalisation of the India 2020 Vision. We shall discuss it in a little detail later. In fact, there were reasons that he did not want to continue in this position. He was a scientist who had undertaken projects and had ensured that they all were taken up and finished within the definite timeliness; this was the way he loved to work. As the PSA, he had finalised the programmes like PURA and India 2020; but he felt that his powers in them were limited and were limited to coordinating and advisory role, while the myriad of government departments involved in them did not give these programmes due priority. Each of these programmes needed the support of several departments, which had their own priorities. For example, interlinking of different rivers needed the support of different ministries dealing with water resources management, agriculture, rural development, *Panchayati raj* as well as different state governments; and all of these did not hold uniform views on these vital programmes. As he lacked authority to make these departments and ministries to initiate work, there was no possibility of these programmes being accomplished in a foreseeable future. This led him to take up an assignment with the Anna University. How motivated he was to interact with children can be found by the fact that during this short tenure, he met over 60,000 students and young people to motivate them for nation-building.

Not many months had passed when there was stir in his life again.

□

10

Ascent to the Rashtrapati Bhavan

The President of India is the highest office in the country; this is more related to respect than power, though he is also the supreme commander of the armed forces. After his retirement, Dr. Kalam joined the Anna University as a Professor of Technology for societal transformation. Later, joining the university in this capacity was described by him as the sixth turning point in his life, which shows what type of importance he attached to teaching. He was, however, destined not to continue with his aspired job. Being President was the last thing on his mind. He had never imagined himself in this post. Moreover, he wanted to complete those ambitious projects for which he had no time during his government service. He wanted to bring forth the ancient wisdom of the country, etched on palm leaves by digitalising it.

On 10 June, 2002, Dr. Kalam had just finished his class when he was asked to go to the Vice Chancellor's Office as there was a call from the PMO (Prime Minister's Office). "What could it be?" muttered he to himself. Not long after, he was talking to Prime Minister Vajpayee on telephone. The message was this: "The nation wants you as the next President."

Dr. Kalam thanked for the offer and said that he would get back to him in an hour. Vajpayee made it clear that he wanted only a 'Yes' for an answer, and not a 'No'.

In a few hours, Dr. Kalam was announced at the NDA (National Democratic Alliance), candidate for the exalted post. The Congress too found it hard to oppose the candidature of this apolitical, eminent member of the minority community. Some allegations floated in the media that the government had played a clever game to defeat any opposition from the Congress, which was wont to oppose anything from the NDA.

Pramod Mahajan, the Parliamentary Affairs Minister, called him up and asked him when he would like to file his nomination papers. In India, it is a common practice with political leaders, with little or no exception, to file papers at the time which they consider auspicious. Mahajan's question was in this context; he wanted Dr. Kalam to consult his astrologist to decide about the time and date. He appeared to have forgotten that he was interacting with a scientist, whose approach to life was dictated by science and reason, and not superstition. Dr. Kalam quipped wittingly, "It is astronomy, and not astrology, that keeps the world going." For him, the nation was bigger than the individual.

The nation was already his fan, but this type of sincerity, honesty and innocence took people by storm; there was a man here who was quite apolitical, who did not think and act like politicians are used to.

Pramod Mahajan himself visited the Anna University and escorted Dr. Kalam to New Delhi. He stayed overnight at the DRDO guest house, where he had stayed earlier during his stint with the DRDO.

On 18 June, 2002 two sets of nomination papers were filed. He filed the first set in the company of Congress leader led by Sonia Gandhi; and for the second, he was accompanied by Prime Minister Vajpayee and other senior cabinet colleagues.

On 19 June, 2002 he addressed the first press conference in the capacity of being the presidential candidate. By this time, many people in the media tried to split hairs about his being unfit for the high post as he was a scientist and not a politician. Some of them went to the extent of ridiculing him for his strange hairstyle. However, Dr. Kalam remained unperturbed, though he was not a seasoned politician. He adopted his candid and straight style to answer to the hard-hitting journalists. He had not yet studied the implications of being the President, but he offered a clue of his innocent mind when he said that he would consult the constitutional experts whenever he needed to. Referring to the imposition of presidential rule in the states, he said that he would decide upon the issue keeping in mind 'What the people need rather, than what a few people want'. Only a few press conferences result into amicable relation between pressmen and politicians; here was one of them.

It would be worthwhile to mention that the President of India is elected indirectly by an electoral college comprising members of Parliament (members of both Rajya Sabha and Lok Sabha) and legislators from state legislative assemblies (Vidhan Sabhas) as well as union territories.

On 18 July, 2002, Dr. Kalam was elected the eleventh President of India. He was the first scientist to enter this glorious office, mustering 90 per cent of the votes polled. Soon after the notification was brought to him by Pramod Mahajan, he had to face the press conference. He first remembered the doyens of science community: Prof. Vikram Sarabhai, Prof. Satish Dhawan and Prof. Brahm Prakash, all of whom were no more, but had been guiding souls to him. And then he went on to divulge his vision: "I want the country to usher in the comity of developed countries in twenty years."

On 25 July, 2002, history was in the making when a person, born in a remote, little-known village in south India, was escorted by the outgoing President K.R. Narayanan to the Central Hall of the Parliament. He was sworn in by B.N. Kirpal, the then Chief Justice of India, in a glittering ceremony in the presence of dignitaries, and, of course, several people from his native village as well as his friends. The outgoing President was reminiscent of 1982 when he had trusted this man with the missile mission, and today, he was entrusting him with the highest post of the land. After this, he was given the customary ceremonial 21-gun salute, followed by being escorted to the Rashtrapati Bhavan by the President's Bodyguard.

Sky is the limit; if you have faith in your capabilities and if you do your work honestly and sincerely, there is no power on earth that can hold you back from achieving the best possible outcome. Proof was just before our eyes. While people thought in these terms, something else was running in Dr. Kalam's mind. He was looking for avenues where he could prove his worth as the President; he wanted to make his tenure worth remembering.

☐

11

As President of India

Dr. Kalam did not take long to settle down in his new capacity. His secretary was P.M. Nair, who had earlier worked under Dr. Kalam during the SLV-3 project. The country was passing through a difficult stage at this time. Gujarat had suffered a massive earthquake not very long ago, on 26 January, 2001, and as if it was not sufficient, this state suffered another blow, this time man-made when two bogies of a train of *Karsewaks* were burnt down by the minority hooligans, in which fifty-eight passengers were burnt alive. The majority community rose in opposition and communal riots broke out. At this time, Narendra Modi was the Chief Minister of Gujarat. The political bias came to the fore at this time. No one seemed to bother about the burning alive of the *Karsewaks* and everybody lamented about the communal riots. Dr. Kalam sought to set it right. He condemned both incidents. He visited Gujarat, it was for the first time that he left New Delhi after becoming the President. He wanted to heal the wounds of both communities.

Before Dr. Kalam left for Gujarat, it was feared that he would be given a cold welcome; it was hinted by even Prime Minister Vajpayee, who did not want him to go there. Narendra Modi, however, displayed his diplomatic skills, he was present at the airport along with his cabinet colleagues to receive the President; not only this, he led him to different relief camps and riot-hit locations, and apprised him of the actual incident. Dr. Kalam realised that everything was not as it was depicted by the people and media in Delhi. Much of distortion and exaggeration take place by the so-called secular people sitting in their air-conditioned rooms.

This incident also proved that the new President was not going to be a 'silent' spectator to things, he was willing to go out and see the things for himself. His vision could not be dimmed by the vested interests. He wanted to set right the lacunae that crumble our system. In this effort, he visited several places, like Bhopal where the gas victims were undergoing untold misery. He made it clear that the country should not remain a mute witness to the devaluation of human life.

He had a unique idea to solve the communal differences, taking deeper roots in the country. He said that thinking is growth and non-thinking amounts to destruction. When things have come to such a pass, it is necessary for the country to have a second vision, utilising the vitality and strength of the seventy per cent young populace. Therefore, he put forward a second vision, bringing into focus his earlier India 2020 vision. He was of the opinion that the communal and other issues were basically trivial in nature and sprang from sufferings that people underwent owing to government's callous attitude to problem. If these problems were solved, there would not be left any time for people to think in narrow terms, and it would also ensure a better development and progress for people. He had his own insight how the country's problems should be solved. He said that people were not ready to explore and experiment new things, and wanted to remain limited to their primordial limits. They needed to shed their suspicions and doubts and come out with a will to be self-dependent. The country has a duty towards you, but you have the first duty towards the country; the country can do something for you when you have rendered your service to it wholeheartedly. His approach required a new transformation in thinking. He also opined that the prevailing limiting attitude of the people was the result of the centuries of foreign rule in the country, making them forget their glorious past. A new awakening is needed to make them realize that they belong to a superior race that had achieved much more; much of western science is based on the basic concepts developed in the country thousands of years ago.

Dr. Kalam did not intend to be the ceremonial President as this August Office was supposed to be looked at. He refused to hold the Iftar party that had become almost customary for all the former presidents. 'Why should I feed the well-fed people?' he asked succinctly. He instructed to donate the money required for this party to orphanages in the form of food, clothes and other things. Not only this, he donated a sum of one lakh rupees himself for this purpose. He did not wish to change his humble dress and hairstyle, however, he accepted the *bandhgala* coat, with an opening in the front, to suit the majestic office he held now. This type of neck was his thinking, and it came to be called Kalam suit.

Dr. Kalam supported the idea of knowledge society and laid down an idea that later became the *Aadhaar Card*. The UIDAI (Unique Identification Authority of India), was set up seven years later and is an important programme which has resulted into reducing corruption in disbursement of subsidies, identification and other ancillary programmes owing to its integrated approach. The programme has not been implemented well enough else it would have phased out the need for voter ID, ration card, and other types of identities.

Dr. Kalam wanted the focus to be brought on basic issues and problems facing the country, such as education, healthcare, development of science and technology, laying infrastructure, justice to people, agricultural development, industrial growth and the like. He wanted to pay special attention to children. He himself remained a bachelor but he shared profound feelings for them. He said that the country could rest awhile only when its children were progressing and learning well; if their welfare is looked after, if they are allowed to grow optimally, the country need not worry for any other problem. He wanted the benefit of science and technology to accrue to every person in the country, including the poorest. He emphasized that every Indian citizen must have physical, economic, social and environmental access to a balanced diet, including the required quantity of nutrition; when he referred to a balanced diet, he also included safe drinking water in it. He wondered why a large Indian population had to sleep on a hungry stomach when there was enough agricultural production in the country to feed everybody. He saw the role of technology in solving this problem.

Dr. Kalam was not comfortable with the fact that India reeled with about world's one-fourth poor people; he wondered how the country could not solve the basic problems despite several decades after independence. He made efforts to seek the cooperation of the concerned department to eradicate poverty; he identified that poverty, more than anything else, was the main source of discrimination and marginalisation. If you had money, few people would tend to ask which caste or religion you belong to.

In healthcare, he was confident that many of the ills in this sector could be eradicated with the convergence of different technologies, as information, communication, medical electronics and simulation. He was also very concerned about the problems being faced by the disabled and mentally-retarded children. While conferring the National Award for the Welfare of Persons with Disabilities at Vigyan Bhavan, on 3 December, 2002, he said that people with disabilities would definitely like to have a life like any other citizen and participate in all social activities and employment.

What endeared Dr. Kalam to people was his forthright approach to all issues, there was no secret agenda. For example, when he discussed terrorism, he wanted to look at it from a different perspective. He acknowledged that we are living in a more frightful environment today, caused by terrorism. He said that countries should not declare a unilateral war on terrorism, rather they should all come together under the banner of the UN and deal with all forms of terrorism at par. He did not want terrorism to be classified into 'good' or 'bad', or 'favourable' to one country and 'unfavourable' to another. He warned that it is a snake that bites its own master. He also wanted to have a humane touch when dealing with terrorism. He deplored that a lot of innocent lives are get caught in the crossfire and people are killed by terrorists. He asked succinctly, "Will the planet earth at any time see a no-war situation?" He said that the world needs to unite to take on this dreaded menace.

Dr. Kalam emphasized that every person has a right to live with dignity, everybody possesses a distinct quality, that may not be considered remarkable by others, but every person is unique, and this uniqueness should be respected. Opportunities should be available to everybody in educational, vocational and career domains so that everybody can rise himself to the exalted ambition and realise his aspiration.

The welfare of the nation resided in the core of his heart. This spirit was manifested expressly on more occasions than one. When, in 2003, he invited all Governors and Lieutenant Governors of the states to New Delhi and interact with the Prime Minister and other ministers, he advised them to not be limited to their only state, rather take decisions which were in conformance with national welfare and interest. He advised them to render the sage advice to the government, and insisted on wider application of information technology in all spheres of the government.

His bent of mind could be read when he delivered the first address to the nation on the eve of the Republic Day in 2003. It was curiously watched on television by millions of people, especially to see if he towed the line of his predecessors, in which they expressed what the government wanted them to. Avoiding reference to usual topics of secularism, socialism and other related issues, he spoke on the need for a knowledge society, a second green revolution, providing urban amenities in rural areas and introducing technology in all types of government functions. He also laid stress on integration of agriculture and industry, and said that the future of every sphere of national life lay in the development of technology. He called upon the young people to devote more time towards development of software and hardware. He said that the needs of the rising population could be met only through the use of technology.

Dr. Kalam was not the one who liked to stay in the comfort of his majestic presidential residence; he liked to venture out to find different shades of life in the country. By the Republic Day in 2003, he had toured seventeen states, that speaks volumes of his involvement with the people. During these tours, he did not restrict himself to only urban areas and state capitals, rather he also visited rural areas and interacted with a variety of people in order to know about their aspiration and what the government could do for them. According to him, world peace originates from domestic harmony and national integration. You cannot hope for world peace when there is discord and conflict in the country, so he wanted all conflicts to be resolved amicably through dialogues. In this connection, he recited the English translation of a poem by Confucius, the great Chinese philosopher:

"Where there is righteousness in the heart,
There is beauty in the character.
When there is beauty in the character,
There is harmony in the home.

> *When there is harmony in the home,*
> *There is order in the nation.*
> *When there is order in the nation,*
> *There is peace in the world."*

Dr. Kalam knew that the power of democracy comes from the people, and it is mainly in the form of people exercising their right to franchise. This was the reason that he chose to appeal to people to vote in 2004, when the Vajpayee government decided to go for early polls following the party's comfortable victory in a number of states and the 'India Shining' campaign. Just before the first phase of elections, Dr. Kalam chose to go on air and addressed to the people. He said, "By casting your vote for a candidate who in your opinion can represent you in the Lok Sabha, you are sowing the seeds for the creation of a prosperous India, a happy India, a safe India, a secure India, and above all, an India with nobility." He exhorted the people to exercise their right for the candidates who, they thought, were capable to realise their aspirations and ambitions. The image of a beautiful India could be brought into reality only when people shared the democratic process.

While dealing with a question why our politics is partisan, caste- or religion-centred, he said that it was natural for the politicians to look after their vote banks, yet keep them backward so that they could not see the reality. You can befool a person for all times, you can befool some people for some time, but you cannot befool all people for all the time. If all people vote, the politicians will have no option but to think in terms of the entire nation as a whole, and not in terms of a particular caste or religion. This is the reason that all people must vote, and it is also equally important that they vote rising above their narrow considerations of region, caste and religion, or issue.

The general election in 2004 brought defeat for the NDA. Dr. Kalam had a very friendly relation with Vajpayee. He said that the common thing between them was poetry.

These elections also brought a surprise for the nation. No party or alliance had secured a clear majority. The BJP still managed to have a sizeable share of seats, 138 to be precise, retaining its voter base. The Congress had not increased its voter base, but had succeeded to jump from 114 in 1999 to 145 in 2004. When the Parliament is hung, the President assumes a greater role. This was a testing time for Dr. Kalam to display his virtuous decision-making.

On 18 May, Mrs. Sonia Gandhi and Dr. Manmohan Singh met Dr. Kalam and apprised him that they had the support of a number of parties. The President informed them that he had already received letters of support from the SP (Samajwadi Party) of Mulayam Singh and RLD (Rashtriya Lok Dal) of Ajit Singh, yet the Congress still fell short of the required number of seats to form the government. It was obvious that her government would have to be dependent on the outside support. Dr. Kalam felt that the Congress could form the government, so he asked them to meet in the evening with letters of support.

The meeting was held in the Rashtrapati Bhavan again in the evening. Mrs. Sonia Gandhi came with Dr. Manmohan Singh, who had also brought the required letters of support. Convinced with this, Dr. Kalam said that they could form the government and the swearing-in ceremony could be held at the time of your choice. When Dr. Kalam said the words 'at the time of your choice', he remembered the 'auspicious time', incident when he himself had filed the nomination papers for the highest post in the country.

There was a surprise in Mrs. Sonia Gandhi's assertion that she would like to nominate Dr. Manmohan Singh instead. At this time, the 'foreign origin', was a hot issue, and the Congress could not take any risk; moreover, Dr. Manmohan Singh had a clean image that the government could safely sail through the parliamentary sessions. This was how the letter appointing Dr. Manmohan Singh as the

Prime Minister and inviting him to form the government was issued.

Finally, Dr. Kalam administered the oath of office and secrecy to Dr. Manmohan Singh and his colleagues on 22 May. The ceremony was held in the Ashok Hall of the Rashtrapati Bhavan, attended by a galaxy of Indian luminaries from different fields, especially politics.

Dr. Manmohan Singh did not enjoy majority of his own in the party, yet it was believed that he would be able to put India on the path to progress and development, especially owing to his past experiences as the finance minister and earlier being the governor of the Reserve Bank of India, deputy chairman of the Planning Commission as well as chief economic advisor. We can recount that the first UPA tenure was somewhat satisfactory, with some cases of corruption, but the second UPA tenure turned out to be a very sore one which sealed the fate of the Congress in the general elections held in 2014, when it was reduced to a paltry 44 seats. It was mainly due to the cases of demonic corruption cases as well as inefficiency. Moreover, the country was embracing itself with the new charisma of Narendra Modi as the Prime Ministerial candidate for the NDA.

The inefficiency of the UPA, and to some extent problems of the later NDA regime, can also be attributed to the dilemma that the Indian way of democracy presents. The party or alliance forming government in the Lok Sabha does not necessarily enjoy majority in the Rajya Sabha, where the opposition party or parties have a say. It disables the party in the Lok Sabha find it hard to pass the bills in the Rajya Sabha, though it has been given the mandate to rule. We have seen it during the UPA regime and during the regime of Narendra Modi, the Congress seems bent to wreak equal and reactionary vengeance upon the NDA. This is the reason that a debate has sparked off about the need for the existence of the Rajya Sabha, that was basically thought of as a house of elders, but it seems to have become a house of politics.

Any way, Dr. Kalam was going strong as the President. He appeared to be a ray of hope for the common people of India; this is proof enough from the large number of letters and e-mails he received daily. Dr. Kalam had personal bond with Azim Premji, the richest Indian at that time. He convinced him to found the Azim Premji Foundation, a non-profit organisation, dedicated to achieving quality universal education. This foundation has worked in the field of elementary education rendering quality assistance to lakhs of government-run schools in rural areas providing basic infrastructure.

In the capacity of being the President, Dr. Kalam visited a lot of places in the country and abroad. He interacted with a large number of people, functionaries, leaders and government representatives from across the globe, and left a positive impression on them.

Dr. Kalam was very reminiscent of his meeting with Nelson Mandela, who had suffered in jail for 27 years for the sake of democracy and anti-apartheid movement. The two instantly struck harmony. Dr. Kalam found him, 'a bundle of cheerfulness'. It was a rare sight to see Nelson Mandela coming out to see off Dr. Kalam, and while walking, he took Dr. Kalam's shoulder as the support discarding his walking stick. When Dr. Kalam asked him about the greatest pioneers of the anti-apartheid movement, Mandela is reported to have said, "There were many, but one of the greatest pioneers of the freedom movement was M.K. Gandhi. India sent us a righteous barrister. We returned him to you as Mahatma Gandhi."

Dr. Kalam was a votary of world cooperation on several issues. He was firm in his view when he said that the problems of the world could not be solved by any one country in isolation. The world experienced shortage of potable water, pollution and depletion of fossil materials and other natural resources. All people of the world did not get equal opportunities for progress. The condition was so bad for some peoples and countries that they did not get even stomachful of food, let alone other amenities of life. Dr. Kalam emphatically said that one or a few countries becoming developed would not solve the problem of the humanity; all countries would have to come together to eradicate the problems facing the people. He was very concerned about terrorism. He clearly said that all countries will have to cooperate if a viable solution to it can be found; it is beyond the power of any one country to tackle it all alone. Time has shown that he was right to say so. The countries, acting alone, have found it hard to curb it, so world leaders today talk of international cooperation, though much needs to be done as yet. Some countries continue to be the sore points of terrorism, such as Pakistan, Syria, Iraq and others. The threat of terrorism can be tackled by a multi-pronged approach, not by the 'fighting approach' alone, because it has in its base several problems including psychology, fundamentalism, social injustice, lack of education, lack of development and the like.

He was very anxious that the big problems of the people of India could not be solved adequately even after so many decades since freedom. He emphasized to develop a new model of an enlightened society which will solve problems, bring prosperity, resulting into the realisation of peace and harmony, not in the country alone, but in the whole world.

Dr. Kalam had always in his arsenal an element of surprise. When in 2005, Pervez Musharraf, President of Pakistan, visited India, and called on Dr. Kalam, everybody hoped that he would talk about terrorism and the role of Pakistan in inciting it. However, even Musharraf was taken aback when Dr. Kalam instead gave a 30-minute-long presentation on rural development; he presented this aspect which could be tackled jointly by the two nations. Musharraf had no words of praise for this presentation. He only said at the end, "Mr. President, India is lucky to have a scientist President like you."

Turmoil

Article 356 of the Constitution of India has always been a bone of contention, under which the President's rule can be imposed in a state. What a President is supposed to do in normal times is to abide by the advice rendered by the Council of Ministers. These two factors brought much discomfort to Dr. Kalam. Let us elaborate.

The elections for the Bihar legislative assembly (Vidhan Sabha) were held in February 2005, in which no party or alliance was able to secure a majority, and none of them was able to form the government with even the outside support of some other party or parties. Mr. Buta Singh was the Governor of the state at that time. He explored all possibilities on the formation of the government, but the numbers did not allow him to take a decision; a stable government could not be imagined at that point of time. When exhausted of all options, he recommended the imposition of the President's rule in the state. With this, the legislative assembly was put in suspended animation. The Cabinet, on 7 March, 2005, recommended the same to the President, who signed the proclamation under Article 356 on the same day. Both houses of the Parliament approved the proclamation the same month.

All this while, the politicians tried to subvert the democratic process and tried to take undue advantage of the provisions in a bid to form the government. This became a curious case. The Governor reported on 21 May, 2005 that the JDU (Janata Dal – United) was involved in horse-trading to form a breakaway faction of the LJP (Lok Jan Shakti Party) MLAs so that it could manage a majority somehow in a bid to form the government. The Governor was of the view that this was an attempt to distort the verdict of the people, and that the assembly should be dissolved instead of it continuing in suspended animation, so that the people could get an opportunity to exercise their mandate afresh and a stable government could be formed in the state. This issue was being debated in the media hotly.

On the very next day, that is, on 22 May, the Cabinet endorsed the assessment of the Governor, and recommended to the President for issue of a presidential order for dissolution of the legislative assembly under Article 174(2)(b) of the Constitution.

At this time, Dr. Kalam was in Moscow, Russia. P.M. Nair, his secretary, in his book *The Kalam Effect*, has provided the details what happened there. When Prime Minister Manmohan Singh informed Dr. Kalam telephonically about this decision and what should be done at his end, Dr. Kalam called his secretary and asked about the further course of action, who advised to wait for the papers. Not long after, the papers were faxed to him containing the Governor's report and the Cabinet's recommendation. The two discussed the matter for quite some time. The secretary advised him to sign the proclamation, and Dr. Kalam did his bidding.

Many people rose to question the wisdom of Dr. Kalam so far as this decision was concerned. Many people even questioned if a scientist was capable enough to tackle such matters or take political decisions; they simply forgot that being a scientist in government service also gives sufficient exposure to diplomacy and administrative experience. Moreover, the President is supposed to follow the advice of the Council of Ministers.

The Proclamation was contested in the court, and the Election Commission started the process for re-election in the state of Bihar. The Supreme Court heard the case in a five-judge bench. A powerful argument put forward was made by Soli Sorabjee on behalf of petitioners (Nitish Kumar and BJP MLAs), who said that the Governor made no genuine attempt to explore the possibility of forming a government before recommending the dissolution of the House. The 'indecent haste', with which the Governor acted would show that his only intention was to prevent Janata Dal (U) leader Nitish Kumar from staking his claim to form the government, as it did not suit the political ambitions of Rashtriya Janata Dal Chief Lalu Prasad. There was no explanation by the Government for the hurry shown in getting the Proclamation signed by the President (who was then in Moscow) at midnight.

The Supreme Court agreed that the Proclamation dated 23 May, 2005 was a unique case. It also observed that the earlier cases that came up before the court were those where the dissolutions of the assemblies were ordered on the ground that the parties in power had lost the confidence of the House; however, in this case, even the first meeting of the legislative assembly had not been convened. Rather, its dissolution had been ordered on the ground that, 'attempts were being made to cobble a majority by illegal means and lay claim to form the government in the state and if these attempts continue, it would amount to tampering with the constitutional provisions'. The Supreme Court specifically asked if it was permissible to dissolve the legislative assembly even before its first meeting had been held, if the dissolution was illegal and unconstitutional, if the *status quo ante*, as on 7 March, 2005 or 4 March, 2005, was to be given, and if the Governor acted within the powers given under Article 361.

The majority judgement by the Supreme Court was seen as a major embarrassment to the UPA (United Progressive Alliance) government at the centre, which recommended the dissolution on the basis of two reports sent by Governor Buta Singh on April 27 and May 21. The bench said that both the petitioners and the Union Government addressed many intricate and important questions of law having a far-reaching impact. It finally said, "Keeping in view the questions involved, the pronouncement of judgement with detailed reasons is likely to take some time and, therefore, at this stage, we are pronouncing this brief order as the order of the court to be followed by detailed reasons later."

The Bench said, "Despite [the] unconstitutionality of the impugned Proclamation, having regard to the facts and circumstances of the case, the present is not a case wherein exercise of discretionary jurisdiction *status quo ante* deserves to be ordered to restore the Legislative Assembly as it stood on the date of Proclamation, March 7, when it was kept under suspended animation."

The Supreme Court finally declared unconstitutional the May 23 Presidential Proclamation dissolving the Bihar Assembly but gave its nod for the present elections, the first phase of which was scheduled for October 18. In its harshest observation, the Supreme Court observed, "...in the absence of the relevant material, much less due verification, the report of the Governor has to be treated as the personal *ipse dixit* of the Governor. The drastic and extreme action under Article 356 of the Constitution cannot be justified on mere *ipse dixit*, suspicion, whims and fancies of the Governor."

The only solace that Dr. Kalam could draw from the judgement was that the court had indicted the Governor, and he had not been named anywhere, though the media called in question his wisdom to sign the papers at midnight without having sought constitutional or legal advice from the Supreme Court, for which he is very much eligible, and he could have waited for some time, at least until his return from Moscow.

Dr. Kalam was an honest and straightforward person. This type of judgement by the Supreme Court was not to his liking, because he had acted *bona fide* on the advice of the Council of Ministers, though he had omitted to take a legal advice in the matter. He was also of the opinion that the government had not satisfactorily presented his side of the case in the court. Nonetheless, the Supreme Court is Supreme that had placed the responsibility on the Governor and to some extent on the government. Still, Dr. Kalam was wont to take responsibility for this. He wrote in his book *Turning Points*, "After all, the Cabinet is mine and I have to take the responsibility."

When Dr. Kalam felt that fingers were being pointed to him, he felt very unhappy. He wrote a letter of resignation, signed it and kept it ready to be sent to the Vice President, Bhairon Singh Shekhawat, who was out of Delhi at that time. Meanwhile, the Prime Minister met Dr. Kalam in connection with some other matter, and at the end of the discussion, Dr. Kalam informed him about his decision to resign; he even showed him the letter of resignation. The PM was taken aback at this revelation.

Dr. Manmohan Singh tried to persuade him that he should reconsider the issue, as it could put the government in a serious trouble, and it could lead to the fall of the government.

Dr. Kalam felt that he needed to consult somebody, so he consulted none else but his own conscience. He wrote in his book *Turning Points*, "I had only one person to consult, and that was none other than my conscience. Conscience is the light of the Soul that burns within the chambers of our heart. That night I did not sleep...asking myself whether my conscience is important or the nation is more important...Then I took the decision to withdraw my decision to resign and not disturb the government."

Dr. Kalam decided to put the matter behind him and look forward to make his remaining tenure as the President fruitful and dignified. His love for young people and children continued unabated. Speaking to students at Jadavpur University, he said: "Education is not merely a tool for development of individuals; it must include the interests of the community and the aspects of nation building. Good education is indeed the foundation for our future...it is empowerment to make choices and emboldens the youth to choose and chase their dreams which must be taken by the universities."

The Pilot and Sailor

Dr. Kalam wished to be a pilot first, but could not. And now, as the Supreme Commander of the armed forces, he wanted to fulfil at least his dormant wish to fly in an aircraft. But he got a chance to sail in a submarine rather early. When you fly or sail in fighting machines like fighter aircraft or submarines, you have to face the rigours, which are suited to a person still young and sturdy. However, Dr. Kalam was aged 75 when he sailed in the submarine: INS Sindhurakshak.

In February 2006, Dr. Kalam visited the port city of Visakhapatnam to review the Indian Navy's fleet and witness its operational prowess. During the submarine's deployment, he was given a demonstrative excursion, during which the submarine dived and sailed in the Bay of Bengal. With Dr. Kalam, accompanied by Arun Prakash, the Chief of the Naval Staff, and Commander P.S. Bisht, the submarine travelled about five miles off the coast and dived to a depth of 50 metres, and did some manoeuvres. He was also taken to the five compartments of the craft, so as to give him first-hand knowledge of the operations. This was followed by the inspection of the ten warships.

On 8 June, 2006, Dr. Kalam realised his childhood dream of being a pilot, albeit for a day. He flew in the SU-30 MkI fighter aircraft with Wing Commander Ajay Rathore. The aircraft took off from the Lohegaon Air Force Base in Pune, for a forty-five minute sortie, in which it went as high as 7.5 km flying at a wonderful speed of 1.25 mach. It was not a simple flight, all the manoeuvres were undertaken, like diving, shooting, stalling, twisting and turning, as he wanted to know about the capability of the aircraft. It was a first-hand experience for him. He became the first President to fly in a fighter aircraft. When he landed, his laughing face said it all how he had enjoyed it.

Journalists questioned if he had felt afraid before the flight. Dr. Kalam smiled in his natural way and said, "There is no living being that is not afraid when it faces danger. True courage is in facing danger when you are afraid."

Fearlessness is about doing something you are afraid of. Recalling his childhood ambition, Dr. Kalam said that he wanted to fly, he had a dream to fly, but he could not be selected for short-service commission in the Indian Air Force, and this brought to an end his wish to fly in a fighter aircraft. He finally got the chance to fly when he was old and then the President of India. When asked again if he felt fear during the flight, he said: "I was so busy with instruments that I didn't have the time to fear about anything." With such a spirit, you are sure to conquer any obstacle, anything that forms fear in the psyche.

Office of Profit Controversy

Gift may be a source of pleasure when it comes to personal bonding between brother and sister, father and daughter, friend and friend, and others; but when it is given or taken with some motive behind it, it becomes a source of corruption; it puts the acceptor under an obligation, as we all are well aware that bribes are given and taken in the name and form of gifts. Dr. Kalam quotes a verse from the *Hadith* which means "Gifts accompany poisonous intentions."

Before we get into the office of profit controversy, let us narrate a story from his early life, and know what important lesson he had learnt from his father.

When Kalam was studying in the Schwartz, he visited his native village during holidays. He was sitting in the courtyard when a stranger came and enquired for his father, who was away. The stranger had brought some gifts for his father. Kalam thought to consult his mother, but she was offering prayers. At this, he said that the newcomer could keep the packet on the cot and leave. When his father returned, he noticed the packets and enquired about them. Kalam told him about the stranger. His father normally never lost his cool, but at this moment he was at once furious. He beat Kalam for his folly. Later, when he regained control over himself, he said, "Abul, when you accept gifts, you come under an obligation to reciprocate, and this is the source of corruption. Never ever accept the thing for which you are not eligible."

Kalam had grown through his career and followed this teaching all his life. But at this turn of life, he was confronted with a situation which needed to be tackled in the right earnest. We are talking about the office of profit controversy. It turned out to be the most dramatic event of his term as the President. Normally, a President is considered to be a 'rubber stamp', who is supposed to follow the diktats of the Council of Ministers; however, this incident proved that he was not susceptible to political pressures so easily and he could remain committed to ethics despite all the hullabaloo.

The Parliament (Prevention of Disqualification) Act, 1959 stipulates that certain offices of profit under the government shall not disqualify the holders thereof for being chosen as, or for being, members of Parliament. However, the politicians, in pursuance to their vested interests, had expanded the horizons of this act and occupied several offices which could have resulted into their disqualification as MPs.

In 2006, Dr. Kalam received a number of complaints from MPs about certain fellow members holding offices of profit which warranted disqualification. He studied these complaints and, learning from his past experience in the case of Bihar assembly dissolution, sent these complaints to the competent authority for advice as well as enquiry; in this case, the Election Commissioner. As the complaints pertained to a prominent member (Mrs. Jaya Bachchan), a lot of fingers started to be pointed out at the President. In accordance with the opinion received from the Election Commission, Dr. Kalam issued a disqualification order against Mrs. Jaya Bachchan.

India knows how our most politicians behave. Different parties oppose each other even on issues of national interests if their vested interests clash, but they show unprecedented unity on issues in which the interests of all of them are at stake. This was one such case. This has become a common practice to offer plum positions to legislators to retain them in the party and coalition, and this practice has become a tool of curbing political dissidence. When Mrs. Jaya Bachchan was disqualified, there was danger of disqualification over several other MPs and MLAs across the country, affecting all political parties. The BJP lost no moment in dragging the position of Mrs. Sonia Gandhi as the Chairperson of the National Advisory Council of the UPA into controversy. In response, she resigned from her Lok Sabha seat and sought re-election.

Meanwhile, the matter of Mrs. Jaya Bachchan was promptly taken to the Supreme Court, contending that she had received no payment in her capacity as the Chairperson of the Uttar Pradesh Film Development Council. The Supreme Court turned down this plea and stated that a member of the legislature holding such an office provided valid grounds for disqualification irrespective of the fact whether he/she received any compensation or payment *in lieu thereof*.

To save the skin of such offenders, the Parliament passed the Office of Profit Bill seeking to exempt fifty-six posts, including that of the National Advisory Council, from being considered offices of profit, and sent it to the President for approval. The very purpose of the bill was to allow the legislators to enjoy more than one position without facing any threat of disqualification. This type of bias has often been observed on part of legislators on several occasions. This has also been the reason that people say that the legislators should not be allowed to legislate a bill in which their own interests clash, and this seems to be a justifiable demand. People's demands are kept pending over years while the legislators keep on making the legislative assemblies and houses of Parliament places of din and noise, but show unprecedented unity when any bill is brought up curbing or extending their rights. This is mockery of democracy.

Owing to such reasons, Dr. Kalam wanted that he should not commit a blunder on this count and probity should be followed. However, the Constitution has bound his hands into certain behaviour, and he could not flout its command. He received the bill for approval on 25 May, 2006, and he returned it on 30 May, 2006 for re-consideration by Parliament; for this, he gave three grounds: first, the bill could not be put into force from a retrospective date; second, there was need to define transparent criteria for exemption from disqualification; and lastly, the bill should be made applicable to all states.

Dr. Kalam was lauded for taking this ethical and legal stance. He has written in his book *Turning Points*, "...I did not find a systematic approach towards deciding the question of what constituted an office of profit. Instead exemption was given to only the existing offices which were occupied by MPs. I also discussed the anomalies and my concerns with three former chief justices of the Supreme Court." This shows that this time, he acted wisely. He wanted the bill to be 'fair and reasonable' as well as 'clear and transparent'. He was right to do so, I suppose. Why should they amend the Constitution of India merely to look after the interests of a few individuals? It was a pertinent question.

As the issue broke out in the media, it was debated for long. Extensive articles were written. Meanwhile, Dr. Kalam was put under tremendous pressure to sign the bill; and this pressure came not from the party whose members were under the threat of disqualification, it came from almost all political parties.

The Parliament considered the bill again, and passed it without any amendment and sent it to Dr. Kalam on 1 August for approval.

Dr. Kalam did not like to keep the things pending. Normally, he sent the bills the very following day of its receipt, but he was taking time in this connection. Prime Minister Manmohan Singh met him to enquire why the bill took so much time for his assent. Dr. Kalam apprised him that he anticipated some action by the Parliament, and he was waiting for it. The Prime Minister informed him that the Parliament had already decided on the constitution of a JPC (Joint Parliamentary Committee), to go into all details of the bill.

Dr. Kalam was being pressurized to pass the bill immediately and was being criticised for the delay; however, he stuck to his ground that the minimum requirement must be met before he signed the bill.

Dr. Kalam was on a tour to the north-east when he received a message that the Parliament had formed a JPC on this bill. This was the action that he was waiting for. He immediately signed the bill.

After a few months, the Parliament approved the recommendation of the JPC, but it did not address the problem as Dr. Kalam had pointed out. He felt that, 'the highest body of the nation is promoting wrong practices'. He rued that the Parliament was not paying serious attention to the bills they deserved and was compromising on probity.

Dr. Kalam thought that the Indian political and bureaucratic systems have been conditioned to maintain the *status quo*, and those in power have found and evolved ways to stay in power, through means foul or fair. He gave this sentiment his voice when he addressed the nation on the eve of the Republic Day in January 2007; he said that instead of 'being driven by what the system can give you', you have to ask 'what you can give'. Our country will make unprecedented progress only when you think in terms of giving to the nation rather than taking from it. He said in his address emphatically, "It will be a reality if everyone 'gives what I can give', through individual, societal and nationwide participation in a national movement facilitated by the government."

Capital Punishment

Dr. Kalam never shied away from his duty, in whatever capacity he worked. He never found any task difficult; if it was so, he would make all efforts to make it simple and easy. However, he found one thing particularly difficult, that was to decide on the issue of confirming capital punishment awarded by the courts. The President is required to take the ultimate decision whether the death penalty should be awarded or not. The beauty of our democracy is that every effort is made to save the life of an innocent person. He is given all types of avenues to prove himself innocent and is allowed to exhaust all possibilities by which he could save his life. When Dr. Kalam took over as the President, there were a number of cases pending for Presidential approval. It is a task that 'no president would feel happy about', as Dr. Kalam observed. He did not want to keep these cases pending, at the same time, wanted to ensure from his side that none of the person was victimized. So, he decided to get all these cases examined from the point of view of the extent or gravity of the crime, its intensity and the social and financial status of the awardees. To his surprise, the study revealed that the cases showed social and economic bias. In many cases, the awardee happened to commit the crime out of enmity, and did not have a direct motive. Of course, he found only one case that merited the highest punishment, that was of a lift operator who raped and killed a girl, in whose case he promptly affirmed the sentence.

Dr. Kalam was criticized for keeping the file of Afzal Guru's conviction pending until he demitted the office. Mohammad Afzal, better known as Afzal Guru, was found involved in the December 2001 terrorist attack on the Parliament and sentenced to death by the Supreme Court in 2004. When a person is sentenced to death, this conviction is upheld by the apex court; and normally, he would be hanged unless he is given presidential clemency, for which the convicted person or his relatives have to file a mercy petition. Though the petition is addressed to the President, he does not act on it himself, rather he refers it to the Ministry of Home Affairs for its recommendations, and acts accordingly. So far as the mercy petition of Afzal Guru was concerned, it was received in his office on 3 October, 2006, and it was sent to the MHA the same day. Until President Kalam demitted office on 25 July, 2007, no recommendation had been received back from the Ministry. The President could not have acted without this recommendation. So, there is no point of criticising him on this score.

Dr. Kalam was also concerned that the source of sustenance of the person punished and his family should be found out. He maintains the spiritual stance that we all are creations of God, and doubts if a human system or human being is competent enough to take away the life of a person on whatever grounds.

During his term as the President, Dr. Kalam addressed a wide variety of meetings, conferences and seminars, including the Parliaments of different countries, including the European Parliament.

As Dr. Kalam's term as the President of India drew to a close, he had decided that he would not like to contest for the second term; during his presidentship, he had been a peripatetic president who visited almost all states of India, often more than once. Now, he looked forward to going back to the job he liked most: teaching, writing and inspiring the youth in national and international schools and universities, and participating in seminars and conferences. He had offers from a number of prestigious educational institutions of the country for a teaching assignment, which included the Anna University, Chennai; IIIT Hyderabad; G.B. Pant University of Agriculture and Technology, Pantnagar; Delhi University; IIM Ahmedabad; IIM Indore; IIT Kharagpur; Benaras Hindu University among others.

The Election Commission issued the notification for the presidential election on 16 June, 2007, which was to be held on 19 July the same year.

The UPA (United Progressive Alliance), led by the Congress, declared Smt. Pratibha Patil, then the Governor of Rajasthan, as its candidate for the highest post. She also enjoyed the support of a few other parties, including the Left parties, BSP and DMK. However, perhaps Dr. Kalam had been the most popular leader as the President until then, so a lot of people wished him to contest for the second term. This line was towed by a number of regional parties, such as AIADMK, SP, TDP, INLD; these parties formed a common front called UNPA (United National Progressive Alliance), and met Dr. Kalam on 20 June, 2007 to convince him to stand in the election. However, Dr. Kalam did not wish to continue, he thought that he had done his part, and he wanted to do something that could contribute to the country's progress, that was to motivate the young people. So, he put a condition which could not be fulfilled; he said that he could stand for the election if it were an unopposed contest. Two days later, he spoke his mind. He said that party politics had never been his domain, and he could not imagine a President seeking votes for his re-election; it would amount to damage the name of the highest post.

In the elections, held as scheduled, Mrs. Pratibha Patil emerged victorious, while the NDA nominee (Bhairon Singh Shekhawat, then Vice President) came second.

Last Speech as President

The members of Parliament hosted a farewell for Dr. Kalam on 23 July, 2007. Addressing the gathering, he spoke of the issues that needed to be looked after by the representatives of the people. He called on them to help people realize their Fundamental Rights, national unity, national security as well as help the nation to progress. He said that the Parliament was faced with greater challenges than ever before since its creation, especially, 'on matters related to human development and governance'. He wanted to transform this institutional instrument of governance. He reminded the parliamentarians the need to tackle the challenges posing threat to national sovereignty, integrity and economic growth coherently and rapidly. He said that the institutions tend to deteriorate with time, resulting into crisis; he pointed out that the Indian system of governance had entered a phase of crisis, and needed self-renewal and change, which could not be accomplished without a spirit of self-sacrifice and justice. Change is the law of nature, and he advised them to go for change if needed, and not rest satisfied with the past developments. He said that it was the ripe time, to 're-energise and give a new charter of life to our public institutions'. He pointed out that public services needed to be improved in the fields of education, health, water and transport. He said that people were not entirely happy with the way the Parliament was functioning, and it needed improvement in terms of accountability. He said that the procedures of the Parliament have to be improved as per the prevailing times. He also stressed the need for rewarding the individual MPs doing good work in order to enhance the incentives for good parliamentary performance. The Parliament has to take a holistic view encompassing all factors of national life.

In political plane, Dr. Kalam put forward a number of suggestions. He was particularly specific pointing out to destabilizing tactics by small political parties. He said that

As President of India

if a small political party, say with less than 10 or 15 per cent of seats in the Lok Sabha, chooses to support the government, and then thinks to withdraw its support, it should be disqualified, because it leads to blackmailing the entire system. He also advocated that all parties in a coalition should function under the banner of a single parliamentary party for the purposes of parliamentary business. He wanted improvement in functioning of ministers, and said that the ministries should set annual targets and the ministers should be held responsible for their actual performance.

Dr. Kalam wished through his suggestions that the parliamentary functioning would improve. Regular boycotts and adjournments have made the entire nation suffer. So, he proposed that public funding of elections should be introduced and a parliamentary act should be passed that neither house can be adjourned more than twice a week unless the listed business has been completed. He also wanted that counting of votes should be made compulsory, and the Speaker/Chairman should be empowered to suspend or expel those members who frequently disrupt the House.

If we see his suggestions in today's parlance, we can find the worth of his suggestions. The Parliament is disrupted over flimsy grounds and even important bills are passed without substantial discussion. This situation has made a mockery of the entire business.

Dr. Kalam also gave a number of suggestions so far as administration of the country is concerned. His suggestions pertained to matters of internal security, development programmes, anti-poverty programmes, integrated appointment to public offices, governmental reforms, corruption and reform of the legal system. He encouraged the parliamentarians to play a more active role in planning and implementation of socio-economic missions. He also deplored that projects are inaugurated but their finish remains a distant dream. He said that it must be ensured that the projects are completed in the given time frame, especially in view of the financial issues.

Dr. Kalam has been a votary of the India 2020 Vision to realize a developed India, so he spoke for providing opportunities for innovation in every aspect of governance and legislative actions. He advised to take into account the 'full advantages and implications of technological revolutions, national and global connectivities, globalization and international cooperation and competition'.

Interactive President

Over the past few years, we have seen the benefits of e-governance; but it was Dr. Kalam who initiated steps for it in the Rashtrapati Bhavan. This helped different echelons of the government contact each other in real time despite one or both being outstation. When he signed the Office of Profit Bill, he was flying to Guwahati. This helps the ministers and officials usefully employ their time when they are travelling.

A high point of Dr. Kalam's presidency has been his interaction. He interacted not only with the Governors and Lieutenant Governors, but also chief ministers, central ministers, MPs, MLAs, and, of course, people, especially young people and students. He provided a platform to people by which people could contact him and write or interact with him on any issue under the sun. Owing to his spirited favour to interaction, he came to be called the 'Interactive President' or 'People's President'.

Dr. Kalam did not meet anybody without having done his homework. He was always clear what he had to do in a certain meeting and what the objective of it was. He says, "Personally, I relished every moment of these meetings." These meetings and inputs from various quarters helped him zero in on his objectives in a better informed way. As a result of such meetings, he started to address professionals, business leaders and researchers on how they can contribute

with innovative ideas to achieve the given objectives. He classified the objectives into ten pillars, which he has mentioned at different places. From these pillars, we get cues about his mind. These ten pillars pertain to the following points:
- Reducing the difference between rural and urban amenities.
- Equitable distribution and adequate access to energy and quality water.
- Agriculture, industry and service sectors should work in harmony.
- No meritorious candidate should be denied education with value-system because of societal or economic discrimination.
- The country should become the best destination for the most talented scholars, scientists and investors.
- The best of healthcare should be available in the country.
- The governance should become responsive, transparent and free from corruption.
- There should be no poverty, illiteracy and crimes against women and children, and no sense of alienation should prevail in anyone.
- The country should become prosperous, healthy, secure, peaceful and happy, following a sustainable growth path.
- The country should become the best place to live and should be proud of its leadership.

Dr. Kalam was of the view that if everybody did his job well enough, the country could improve, and he emphasized this point every now and then. He quoted Shakespeare in an interaction with students, saying "They also serve who stand and wait", the service of each person is important for the society. Everybody has different roles to play in the national life.

He wrote for his motherland:
"O Mother, Mother India,
You have nursed us and grown us,
And gave us a parting mission
And an eternal message.
O my sons and daughters,
Wherever you go,
Whatever mission you do,
Remember, my children,
My three advices golden!

Always be truthful even in danger,
Sweat and sweat to acquire,
Knowledge and name,
Wherever you live enrich that land."

Feeling anxious about the massive number of court cases in India at every level of judiciary, Dr. Kalam pertinently said that such a situation led to delay in delivering justice; therefore, the number of courts should be increased and posted with adequate number of judicial officers and staff with specialized knowledge. He was particularly harsh at those who followed dilatory tactics seeking frequent adjournments and delays in filing documents. He stressed that the administrative staff of the courts will have to work in tandem with the highest ideas enshrined in the Constitution. He proposed to resolve cases through humane touch, creation of *Lok Adalats* and ensuring alternative dispute redress mechanism. He also said that computerization will also help to expedite cases and justice.

Thus, we see that during his tenure of five years at the helm, Dr. Kalam made significant contribution to his August position. He rose from a popular scientist to the People's President; and this journey was most satisfying. He tried to do his best during the presidency. He led a life of busy schedule. He wanted to achieve much, but he could not do many things because of the system and lack of willingness on part of those involved, because everybody seemed to maintain the *status quo*. Bringing a change seemed to be a very hard nut to crack. Perhaps the finest tribute was paid to him by *The Tribune*, that said: "A glorious presidential term will soon be behind him. A people's president is how he will long be remembered. With no personal axes to grind, he occupied the August office and edifice of presidency with great distinction."

During his stay in the Rashtrapati Bhavan, he was enthralled by the spiralling Mughal Garden. He had it in his mind when he composed a poem, which goes thus:

"My garden smiles,
Welcoming the spring,
Roses, beautiful roses,
With fragrance and beauty,
Ringing tunes of the honeybees
Lovely scene, everywhere
My garden smiles.

The enchanting scene entered into me
Blossomed happiness in my body and soul.
Variety of roses,
One lovely family of roses,
Presiding the dynamic scene,
With pleasant fragrant breeze,
My garden smiles."

Dr. Kalam left the Rashtrapati Bhavan as humbly as he had entered it. It is ego which makes an angel a devil; and it is humility which transforms a moral man into an angel. With his simplicity, warm heart and brilliant mind, he had raised the majestic structure into Glory personified.

□

12

The Job that Kalam Loved Best

At 76 years of age, when most people would think of turning inward and leave the world to its fate and to rest in the glory of the hard work they had done in their working life, Dr. Kalam had no such idea. His mission of life was not yet over. His mission was simple: Do everything to make the young people positive in thinking and motivate them to do their bit for the national welfare. Even if he had wanted to retire, maybe people would urge him to remain active, such a favourite and popular figure he had been. He lived a healthy life, so he showed no sign of fatigue, and was ready to embrace himself with a busy schedule at this turn of life. After demitting the office of the President, he was in ever more demand.

Ever since his early professional life, Dr. Kalam liked to speak to the youth. Perhaps he knew that he was not going to live for many years, so he wanted to achieve his ambition as soon as possible. This was the reason that just three days after he left the Rashtrapati Bhavan, on 28 July, 2007, he was at the IIIT (International Institute of Information Technology), Hyderabad interacting with the students. He called upon students to make a major impact on the social and national life. Going from city-to-city, country-to-country, speaking to people, answering their e-mails and letters, he enjoyed his work greatly. He did not let anything go by chance. He wanted to ensure that everything was done perfectly. He often received letters and presentations in Hindi and other languages. He got them translated of his own. I am fortunate to have translated the Hindi letters addressed to him, which he used to send me. Many of them were very simple, and did not have any worthwhile information, like acknowledgements, yet he did not want to miss the content of any one of them. For him, everything was important, so earnestlg he was to his working.

His style of working was simple, yet goal-oriented, and it won him ever more fans, ranging over all age groups, right from the smallest to the oldest. Wherever he was, he charmed the people with his gait, style of speaking, noble ideas, patriotism and the captivating smile.

Dr. Kalam often insisted on cultivating leadership qualities. For him, a leader ought to possess the following qualities to be a successful leader:

- Be proficient in modern technology so that the maximum work can be undertaken in the minimum time.
- Have a vision; there can be no leader without a vision.
- Travel an unexplored path; if you don't go on the paths yet unexplored, you cannot become a leader; it readies you to take risks and undertake enterprises that would prove useful to you.
- Must know how to manage success, and even more importantly, failure.
- Have the courage to make decisions. Your decisions may prove wrong in hindsight, yet without them, you cannot create a niche for yourself.
- Have nobility in management, be transparent in all your dealings, at every level of personal and professional life.
- Work with integrity; it will make success everlasting.

So far as the use of technology is concerned, he referred to himself and said that it, 'gave me the tools to fight poverty, cut across caste and community barriers and bring pride in performance'. His insistence on development of technology has helped to curbed corruption, though much after he quit office.

Dr. Kalam not only insisted on technology, he stressed that indigenous technology must be developed. Earlier in his life as a scientist, he had helped to shape indigenous technology for many projects like the SLV-3 and missiles. He was confident that the Indians are capable of developing technology, and they can do it at a much lower cost than other nations.

During all his speeches addressed to young people, he focussed on the use of technology and cultivation of positive qualities: honesty, commitment, righteousness, hard work, vision, love. He also exhorted parents and teachers to play a role in inculcating these qualities in the children. He deplored that the lack of these qualities had led the public life to deteriorate over the years, and this could not be allowed to continue. He said that love was the most important factor, whatever name you can give it. It can be parental affection or a teacher's favour, this puts a person on the right path. He stressed that a child should never feel the lack of it at home.

Dr. Kalam continued to do his bit for the government. When the nuclear deal was about to be signed and Dr. Manmohan Singh was even ready to sacrifice his seat, while the people of Kudankulam in Tamil Nadu had risen in revolt against the nuclear plant, Dr. Kalam visited the place to allay their fears. He exhorted them to have a national sense. He said emphatically, "We are all too susceptible to our fears and dangers. Cowardly people cannot make history, it is the brave who bring transformation." It was owing to his visit that the people looked at the nuclear plant more favourably. This also shows his standing among the people and what type of trust and confidence he enjoyed in the country.

In a poem, Dr. Kalam says thus:
"The Nature's citizens inspired,
What can I give?
Yes, removing the sorrow of the needy,
Gladdening the sad heart,
And above all, I realised, in giving
Happiness radiates all around."

What a favourite he was with people can be found out from the incident when the election for the President was due in 2012. While the UPA declared Pranab Mukherjee their candidate for the exalted post, the people and opposition parties wanted Dr. Kalam back to the post. Many politicians met him to persuade him to contest the election; these included Mamata Banerjee, L.K. Advani and Mulayam Singh Yadav. Dr. Kalam, however, would have none of it. He clarified that he had, 'considered the totality of this matter, and the present political situation, and decided not to contest the presidential election 2012'. With this statement, he rested all speculation about his return to the Rashtrapati Bhavan.

☐

13

Influences

There are many shades of Dr. Kalam's personality; the more you explore, the more you find. He has been a towering personality of the Indian nation, with a global impact. Now, we will try to explore some aspects of his personality. We have, in the preceding pages, revealed many shades of his personality. Several incidents and influences have played a role in shaping his personality. We shall try to explore some of these.

Seven Turning Points

There are some moments or incidents in anyone's life that bring about a complete transformation; and the life of Dr. Kalam has not been untouched by them which raised him to newer, higher accomplishments. He could have listed a great many of them, but he vividly recalls only seven of them and calls them turning points of his life.

The first turning point, recalls Dr. Kalam, was when he happened to meet Prof. MGK Menon, and became instrumental to his interview with Prof. Vikram Sarabhai. This is also a lesson for the interviewers as the interview proceeded to explore the possibilities in Kalam rather than looking at his knowledge and skills that he possessed at that time. With this, he was selected as the rocket engineer, and this was the point which transformed his life forever.

The second turning point of his life came when he was appointed the Director, DRDL (Defence Research and Development Laboratory) in Hyderabad. This gave him an opportunity to apply space rocket technology to missile technology, and this proved crucial for his career and ambition.

The third turning point came when he took over as the Scientific Advisor to the Defence Minister and Secretary, Department of Defence Research and Development. At this stage, he wanted to join the Madras University as the Vice Chancellor. However, P.V. Narsimha Rao, the then Defence Minister and later Prime Minister, asked him to continue as the Scientific Advisor as he was engaged in a number of important national programmes.

The fourth turning point in his life was when he turned down the offer from Atal Behari Vajpayee for a berth in the Cabinet, and this allowed him to pursue two important national programmes: induction of the Agni missile and five nuclear tests in 1998.

The fifth turning point of his life was when he was appointed the Principal Scientific Advisor to the Government of India in the rank of a Cabinet Minister, and allowed to pursue India 2020 Vision.

The sixth turning point in his life was his appointment as the professor of technology at the Anna University, as he avidly wanted to enter the field of academics; this might be much contrary to your wish as you could have thought his rise to the President as the turning point, which he does not consider to be so.

And the seventh point is when, after his tenure as the President of India, he returned to a career in academics and research, and continued to work with passion for transforming India into an economically developed nation by the year 2020.

Teacher

Dr. Kalam acknowledges that he is because his teachers moulded him that way. He could not have gone on to attain the glory without the active cooperation of his teachers. The teacher plays an important role in our life. For a small child, he or she is the second mother, and we cannot think of a reformed and delicate personality without the hand of a teacher behind any person. Dr. Kalam too attaches great significance to the teacher. Let us quote him:

"What is education? It is a learning process designed so that it leads to creativity. The result of the educational process is to foster creativity. This comes from the environment in schools and each teacher's capability to ignite the minds of students."

He was very clear about the role that a teacher can play in the national life. He says: "The aim of the teacher should be to build character and human values and enhance the learning capacity of children through technology. They need to build confidence in children so they can think fearlessly and creatively."

Dr. Kalam attaches a great significance to creativity, and says that the teacher can play a very vital role in its realization. However, he also deplores that many a teacher is wont to get transfers to urban areas, which leads to degrading of education in the rural areas. This has compelled the parents, who can afford, to shift, or send their wards, to urban areas for purposes of education, which they ought to get in their remote, far-flung, inaccessible villages. The nation cannot develop fully unless each village is equipped with talent that intends to serve there itself, and this cannot be achieved if teachers do not remain back in villages.

Dr. Kalam has great faith in the teachers and says that they alone can teach us the realities of life, cultivate creativity and eliminate social evils from our social life. He is well aware of the problems that teachers face in this country, but he stresses the need for rediscovering their past glory when they were respected as Gurus. He says:

"Many of them (teachers) work under miserable conditions. We are aware of the need to solve their problems, but even given these, we request that teachers do two things. First, let them think about a developed India in their own ways and enthuse the students. Secondly, they should update their own knowledge because the student is only as good as the teacher."

Books Kalam Loves

Dr. Kalam emphasizes the importance of reading in life, especially if you wish to become successful. Let us quote his words: "Good books become lifelong companions. They enrich our lives and guide us with their undying appeal and ability to talk to multiple generations of readers."

Reading opens vistas of our mind. This is the reason that a number of books have been close to his heart, including *Light from Many Lamps* by Lillian Eichler Watson, *Man the Unknown* by Dr. Alexis Carrel and Thiruvalluvar's *Thirukkural*, a Tamil epic. He has read these books many times over and draws infinite inspiration from them. He credits his success to many aspects of life, including books. He says, "Books can be sources of inspiration for anyone, anywhere." He not only emphasizes reading for its spontaneous and evident benefits, but also exhorts his readers, especially students to recognise the importance of home libraries. He often suggests parents to give their wards the gift of a small library in their own houses with about twenty books to start with to help them cultivate reading habits at an early age. He said that, 'a home library is the greatest wealth'. He thinks very high of reading when he says: "Reading for one hour each day can transform our children into great teachers, leaders, intellectuals, engineers, scientists and most importantly, into thinking adults."

But he does not lose sight of the importance of practice; he warns that we must not sit back in the comfort of our houses going through pages after pages without anything to show on the practical field. Theory has to be matched with practical wisdom; what we learn from books must be transformed into practical ideas that would lead us towards our goals of development; it should exalt our minds towards innovation and adoption of technology in all fields concerning humanity, keeping the national interests at the centre.

Reading has another bright aspect. You can refer to the source of knowledge whenever you are struck during the course of your occupation or discussion with some adversary. Dr. Kalam himself used this quality to overcome his adversary in a discussion with some foreign nationals when they started to discuss the origins of rocketry and Dr. Kalam claimed Tippu (Tipu) Sultan as having possessed the earliest wisdom. When a person pointed out that Tippu had got the technology from the French, Dr. Kalam referred to the book, *The Origins and International Economics of Space Exploration* by Sir Bernard Lovell. It is for sure that he could not have done this had he not widely read.

□

14

Resolving Entanglements

Our country is beset with a number of problems. It is deplorable that even after several decades since our independence, we have not been able to resolve all of them effectively. Many of these problems have become very sour, and need a vision to resolve them. Here are some insights from Dr. Kalam, who presents a viable solution for some of these problems. These are in addition to those which we have discussed during the course of the book.

Ram Janambhoomi-Babri Masjid Controversy

Dr. Kalam is a true visionary; he provides us with easy, pragmatic solutions to difficult problems, the solutions which can be implemented without agonising any souls, while keeping them all satisfied with justice. With such an ease of positive thinking, he provides a solution to the Ram Janambhoomi-Babri Masjid problem that you cannot help but agree with him. He says that people of India have displayed unity of minds and unity of purpose while fighting for freedom, and now is the stage when we must display these qualities in the, 'second national vision which would integrate people from all walks of our society towards a common purpose'. Very emphatically he states:

"The second vision of our nation would transform it from the present status of a developing to a developed nation by integrated actions simultaneously...this vision of the nation will also remove the conflicts arising out of differences and small thinking."

Coming to the Ayodhya problem specifically, he recommends nurturing the cradle of human history and its timeless struggles and triumphs into glory. He says:

"I visualize the holy land of Ayodhya emerging as an unblemished symbol of humanity's quest for service and a beacon of the nation's spirit of harmonious integrity by the year 2020. I envisage Ayodhya to be a Humanity Healing Centre, the founding place for a state-of-the-art multidimensional healing centre, a place which alleviates pain in all forms: physical, mental and spiritual."

He advocates that this healing centre should have four essential features. The first one should be healing in health, which should provide medical services to all people, especially the poor, as good as for free, and it should include the medical systems India presently practices: Ayurveda, Unani, Siddha, Naturapathy and Yoga in addition to Allopathy. The next feature should pertain to the provision of research facilities in different domains of science and technology specifically addressed to resolve the national problems. It should also amalgamate the physical with spiritual healing, and domains should be allotted to different faiths for this purpose. And its fourth feature should pertain to, 'imparting value-based knowledge to people from around the world'. He says:

"It would be crucible for confluence of diverse faiths which would facilitate the youth to imbibe and adhere to values which the nation would be proud of."

Secularism

Secularism is an important feature of the Constitution of India as well as of our country. It was essential to introduce this feature into our Constitution in view of the number of faiths and religions in our country. Dr. Kalam feels proud about this aspect; he describes it in these words:

"A unique source of my pride in being an Indian, since my school days, is that our country is home to all the world's religions and has always propounded and practiced the truth of *Sarva Dharma Sambhav* (equal respect for all religions)."

The Constitution of India emphasizes, time and again, that all people, irrespective of their faith, religion, caste, class or sex, they all enjoy the same rights. He describes this in these words:

"India is a pluralistic society, with equal rights and responsibilities for citizens belonging to people of all religions, regions, castes, classes and linguistic communities."

This is the reason that we Indians feel that the essence of our nationhood lies in secularism. Dr. Kalam condemns any discrimination in the name of religion or faith. He calls it false religion. In his own words:

"Intolerance and violence in the name of religion is the worst form of irreligion. True religion is the Ocean of Spiritualism in which all faiths shine in brilliance. To people in politics and government, it teaches the message of leadership with compassion and fairness."

Dr. Kalam feels that if we all devote ourselves to the ideals of secularism, it is sure that our nation will emerge strong and developed. In his words:

"Here I also wish to reiterate my unflinching commitment to the principle of secularism, which is the cornerstone of our nationhood."

He says that he has become what he is because of the support of people of all religions and faiths and regions. He emphatically says:

"The broad and enthusiastic support I have received from all corners and communities of India is itself a resounding reminder that our secular ethos is alive and vibrant."

Empowerment of Women

Everybody knows what important role women play in our life, yet such a situation has come to be created in which they became a disrespected lot, and Dr. Kalam wants them to have their due, but this can be done by the women themselves, thus, he assigns them the onus of this responsibility. He says that there is need to empower women, but this can be realised when they become conscious of this.

As a consequence of the Fundamental Rights conferred on them, the women in independent India are in a comparatively better position today, but problems still persist. In his words: "Some of the problems, which haunted women for centuries, such as child marriage, practice of 'Sati', prohibition of widow remarriage and discouragement of education for girls have almost disappeared. Developments in the field of science and technology, access to good education and healthcare, and active socio-political movements have further helped to change the attitude of society towards women. These developments have boosted the morale and self-confidence of women."

As a result of these positive changes, an increasing number of women feel that they have an independent individuality, personality, self-respect, talent, capacity and efficiency. However, Dr. Kalam advises that women themselves should come forward and make most of the available opportunities. In his words:

"Women who could utilise the opportunities made available to them have proved that they are as capable as men in discharging the responsibilities assigned to them. However, new situations bring with them new challenges. In some ways, as compared to earlier times, the Indian woman today has to bear a heavier burden of managing the home and her career, which is leading to newer stresses and anxieties."

He advises women to not wait for something big to happen, rather they should start immediately where they are and with whatever they have. He exhorts women in these words:

"You cannot just sit there and wait for people to give you that golden dream, you have got to go out there and make it happen for yourself. Everyone has talent. What is rare is the courage to follow that talent to the place where it leads... Discover who you are, and what is it that you need to do or to be, to feel good about yourself... A woman is indeed the full circle of God's creation and within her is the power to create, nurture and transform."

Black Money

Black money is a raging issue at present, though some steps seem to have been taken, but they all appear far from reality and effect. Black money is also available within the country, but what makes news is the money parked by Indians in tax havens abroad. With so much of hullabaloo about it, there is no consensus on the amount of money deposited abroad, everybody seems to have a different conjecture. Whatever the amount, if the money is retrieved, Dr. Kalam opines, "It could obviously be used to great benefit in core areas like health, education, and housing, pressing issues that need funding on a large-scale to make a difference."

Black money has more influences than seem to come to the fore. It has direct and indirect bearing on our life. Its direct impact can be seen on public finance, economic growth and ultimately the society. Opining on how to curb the menace of black money, Dr. Kalam recommends to bring about some structural changes in the administrative and governance system through measures, such as introduction of a strong *Lokpal Bill*, converting income tax into expenditure tax, bringing out the hidden money out through an amnesty scheme, and so on.

Dr. Kalam appears to have a clear notion how this menace can be curbed. He says that inclusive governance will focus on developing the capabilities of political and economic institutions to perform the increasingly complex and demanding tasks expected of them by enacting policies which will do away with bottlenecks. He wants action to be taken on all three pillars of democratic governance (Legislature, Executive and Judiciary), and three tiers of government (Centre, State and *Panchayat*). Let us quote his own words:

"The capabilities of these institutions to deliver on their mandate need to be greatly improved. The gaps are most evident at the lowest level of principles (*Panchayati Raj* Institutions), where trained personnel are lacking and the training systems are also inadequate. It is also true at higher levels, where trained personnel may be available, but the capability of the systems is poor because they are not performance-oriented and motivation is low."

☐

15
Vision

Dr. Kalam was a visionary. He himself said that a man without vision cannot be better than a beast. He envisioned not only for himself, but for other people and the nation.

Developed India

When we talk of development, most people are inclined to describe it in terms of economic development, in terms of per capita income, gross national product and gross domestic product and related aspects; but this presents only an incomplete picture as all these deal with certain facets of living conditions. Economic development is more in the form of average than the actual condition prevailing on the ground. One in four persons earning a huge sum will make the average look promising, but that would not be the actual case. This is the reason that Dr. Kalam speaks of development in several other aspects, in addition to economic parameter, and these include nutrition, life expectancy, infant mortality rate, availability of sanitation, availability of drinking water, quantum of living space, quality of human habitat, incidence of diseases, dysfunctions, disorders and disabilities, access to medical facilities, literacy, availability of schools and educational facilities, levels of skills, among others. He envisions that a developed India can be achieved only when all these parameters are achieved on the ground. He attaches importance to the strategic interests as well as needs for globalisation. In his own words:

"A developed India should be able to take care of its strategic interests through its internal strengths and its ability to adjust itself to the new realities. For this, it will need the strength of its healthy, educated and prosperous people, the strength of its economy, as well as the strength to protect its strategic interests of the day and in the long-term."

Thus, for him, a developed India is a broad notion encompassing different domains of national, social and personal life, through which all aspirations of the people of India can be realised in realistic terms.

Vision 2020

We have witnessed over the past two decades different prime ministers speak about the need to achieve economic development by the year 2020. As the debate time in the legislatures is curtailed, we can feel the concept of Vision 2020 coming under stress, as petty party politics comes to the fore, and it is not doing anything good to the vision. Dr. Kalam is clear about the Vision 2020 and says in no uncertain terms that this does not belong to a party, a government or an individual, rather it is a national vision. He wishes all elected representatives and other stakeholders to debate, discuss and assent to the national consensus, while slipping the vested interests under the carpet. He wants all people to take part in the discussion, including the executive, the judiciary, the political leaders, the media, the academia, the business people, the medical fraternity, the farmers, the youth and all common people of the country. He has explained what he means by India 2020. Let us quote his own words that he spoke during a lecture:

"Developed India is a Nation where the rural and urban divide has reduced to a thin line; a Nation where there is an equitable distribution of energy and quality water; a Nation where agriculture, industry and service sector work together in symphony, absorbing technology thereby resulting in sustained wealth generation leading to higher employment potential; a Nation where education is not denied to any meritorious candidate because of the societal or economic conditions; a Nation which is the best destination for the most talented scholars and scientists all over the world; a Nation where the best of healthcare is available to all the billion population and the communicable diseases like AIDS/TB, water-and vector-borne diseases, cardiac diseases and cancer are extinct; a Nation where the governance uses the best of the technologies to be responsive, transparent, easily accessible and simple in rules, thereby corruption-free; a Nation where poverty has been totally alleviated, where illiteracy and crime against women are eradicated and where the society is unalienated; a Nation that is prosperous, healthy, secure, peaceful and happy; a Nation that is one of the best places to live in, on the earth and brings smiles on billion-plus faces."

Dr. Kalam feels confident about the fundamentals of the Indian economy and says that it can withstand the global economic crisis to a certain extent, though there remain some areas of concern which can be overcome with devotion and work. To achieve this, he stresses the need for laying down infrastructure as part of rural and urban development missions. He says that the development of means of transport in the form of highways, airports, seaports and railways can ensure the vision to be realised in the times to come. He also aspires to provide other amenities of life under his vision, including clean and green energy, safe drinking water and other needs for all people.

Dr. Kalam lists a number of aspects which have to be realised on the basis of zero poverty, 100 per cent literacy, quality healthcare for all, quality education embedded with value systems for all, and value-added employment for every citizen consistent with education and professional skills. He exudes with confidence when he says:

"If we channelize our integrated efforts towards the development of India before 2020, then the growth of the nation is certain."

Song of India

One young girl, who was often bashed at the hands of her brother living abroad, curiously asked Dr. Kalam, "When can I sing a song of India?"

Dr. Kalam tried to assuage her feelings and explained to her that India 2020 Vision was a step in the right direction and would enable her to sing a song of India by the year 2020. He said that the vision has all the corollaries of taking India forward to advancement. Such positive inspirational lectures by him have led to bring about a positive change in the thinking of the young people, who now are willing to take up the cudgels for their lives rather than being merely dependent on the government to do something for them. They reverberate with the sentiment: "I can do it, we can do it and the nation can do it." Dr. Kalam feels very optimistic. He states:

"With the youth actively participating in the developmental process, I am sure that India will be transformed into a developed nation before the year 2020."

In his poem *Noble Nation*, he writes in verse:
"One of the nations with great civilization,
India 2020 celebrates the birth of the noble nation.
Light of celebration from India reaching our galaxy
Nation with clean environment without pollution,
Having prosperity without poverty,
Peace without fear of writing,
A happiest place to live."

Infrastructure

Infrastructure is like a core competency, it is the

foundation from which we can start to build massive edifice of our national glory. The important factors of laying infrastructure include technology, means of transport, means of communication and electricity generation. Let us quote Dr. Kalam why he emphasizes this need for infrastructure:

"The reason I am emphasizing these aspects is simple. India can launch itself into a developed status only when the economic machinery starts 'real movement', through the infrastructure. Once the machinery moves, the process of economy will create more money in about five to seven years. That money can be reinvested in further improvements."

Technology can be used to bring about value-addition to the products we already possess and to further expand the scope. It also means that we can build infrastructure in new fields with its help, as we did in the field of space exploration.

As our life assumes global proportions, there is increasing need for expansion of means of transport and travel. Railways, roads, waterways and airways have to be built properly, and, at the same time, their quality has to be maintained. This also brings into attention the importance of communication. In the words of Dr. Kalam:

"Both domestic and global economic and physical connectivities (through road, rail, aircraft, ports and airports) depend vitally on telecommunication networking. Instant transfer of information is essential for any business today."

Likewise, electricity generation is like the backbone of our economy, but at the same time, we have to rely on clean sources of energy, like hydroelectricity, biogas plants, solar energy, wind energy and ocean energy.

Dr. Kalam says that laying infrastructure requires large funds, but they can be managed through government as well as private resources. He says that private investment has been coming into India for laying infrastructure, but that is more in the nature of piecemeal fragments rather than being satisfactory. Of course, many other issues remain to be resolved which will boost infrastructure, such as availability of land and government clearances. There can be no other alternative but to improve upon all these components, the sooner the better.

Indigenous Production

Dr. Kalam favours indigenous production and development of everything. He calls this value addition. He says that turning iron ore into steel is value addition; turning steel into a car is value addition; turning cotton into cloth is value addition; and it is value addition when cloth is turned into a garment. India has a large natural wealth, despite this fact India remains a poor country. What happens is that we export iron ore and import the finished goods at a far higher price; and we could have added value to iron ore to earn the profit ourselves, but this does not happen. In such a consequence we have to suffer too; we have to tolerate the whims and fancies of the developed countries on many occasions.

Dr. Kalam recounts an incident when there were needed beryllium diaphragms for the SLV in 1970s. When they tried to procure it from a US company, they were refused this saying that it could be used in the ballistic missiles. You will be surprised to know that beryllium is mined in India, exported to Japan which refines it and exports it to the US, and it was this company that was refusing to give us something that was made from our own ore. Simply but, we have to face the whims and fancies of other nations about something which is our own.

He concludes with a warning: "It is a lesson that must be quickly learnt."

Knowledge Society

Knowledge has always been the prime mover of prosperity and power; therefore, acquisition of knowledge has been the thrust area throughout the world. In India, there has been a culture of sharing it, not only through the tradition of teacher-pupil in the age-old *Ashram* system and medieval education system; and Dr. Kalam does not inhibit himself when he describes the importance of knowledge in unparallel terms. Let us quote him:

"Knowledge has many forms and it is available at many places. It is acquired through education, information, intelligence and experience. It is available in academic institutions, with teachers, in libraries, in research papers, seminar proceedings and in various organisations and workplaces, with workers, managers, in drawings, in process sheets and on the shop floors."

Dr. Kalam favoured to acquire knowledge wherever it might be available. He deplores that ancient India was an advanced knowledge society, but invasions and colonial rule destroyed its institutions and robbed it of its core competencies. By the time the British left, our youth had lowered their aims and were satisfied with earning an ordinary livelihood. He wishes to restore the ancient wisdom. He says that, 'it (India) must rediscover itself in this aspect'. He is sure that once this rediscovery is done, 'it would not require much struggle to achieve the quality of life, strength and sovereignty of a developed nation'.

He is very optimistic that becoming a knowledge superpower is a very important mission for the nation, and he seeks to achieve it sooner than later. To achieve this goal, he seeks to take suitable steps in the fields of education, science, technology and rural development, so that the acquisition of knowledge leads to development in true sense of the world.

When we have developed into a knowledge society, Dr. Kalam opines, there can be no stumbling block to our progress, for knowledge is the foundation on which the highest buildings can be raised.

PURA

Dr. Kalam put forward the vision of PURA (Providing Urban Amenities in Rural Areas) to alleviate poverty in the rural regions. He says that there is need to, 'create sustainable development in the rural areas...and empower the people in the villages with increased employment opportunities, using their traditional core competencies combined with sufficient value addition and necessary skill upgradation, thereby enhancing their per capita income to at least twice the existing level'.

He says that there are a number of projects aimed at attaining sustainable development, but there are threats to health and environment; and, therefore, there is need to enrich biodiversity. He has clear views on how the poor can become the beneficiaries of sustainable development. He points out that using human resources is making the entrepreneurs and vested interests rich who live away from the place of natural resources, while the local populace has to suffer the exploitation of natural resources. He suggests that the convergence of technologies such as biotechnology, informatics, nanotechnology and ecotechnologies offer the hope to initiate sustainable development, and its benefits can be transmitted to the poorer sections through the use of information and communication technology.

Dr. Kalam says in this respect:

"Using information and communication technologies, we need to evolve an innovative societal business model so that the research results of convergence of technologies are used for human development in a sustainable way."

However, he knows that this, 'unique business model, which would empower and enrich the end-users, such as farmers, fishermen, skilled workers, people living in the rural areas, is yet to be evolved'. So, he suggests:

"I suggest eight essential empowerment attributes which are critical to the realisation of our goal of a happy, prosperous and peaceful society beginning at the base of pyramid. These attributes are: access to food and water, access to healthcare, access to income generation capacity, access to education and capacity building, access to quality power and communication applications, state of societal conflict, access to financial services, access to clean and green environment."

To reach the development goals, we have to initiate development works in 6,00,000 villages where seventy per cent of our population resides. Dr. Kalam says:

"Our urban areas have already reached a stage of rapid growth and development. For reaching our villages with equal rapidity, it is planned to be achieved through a rural development programme called Providing Urban Amenities in Rural Areas (PURA)."

This concept consists of four connectivities: physical, electronic, knowledge and consequently to economic. This will help to generate a market and production establishments for servicing the market, leading to prosperity of clusters of villages. He says:

"PURA has all the dimensions to become a business enterprise which has global dimensions but is operating in every nook and corner of our country... PURA entrepreneurs have to have the skill for evolving a business plan with banks and also create infrastructural support, such as educational institutions, health centres and small-scale industries, transportation services, tele-education, tele-medicine, e-governance services in the region integrating with the governmental rural development schemes, such as road, communication and transport and also with national and global markets to sell products and services."

Dr. Kalam prefers to classify PURA into three categories of clusters. Type A cluster is the one situated close to urban areas with limited road connectivity, infrastructure and support. Type B cluster is also located near an urban area but with far less infrastructure, while Type C cluster is located far deep in the countryside with no infrastructure, connectivity or basic amenities. Other categories for this can be, those located near coasts and in the hills.

Dr. Kalam says that small-and medium-sized industry enterprises can undertake management of schools, healthcare units, vocational training centres and other infrastructure, in partnership with banks educational institutions and government and private entrepreneurs.

◻

16
Abiding Values

Dr. Kalam has interacted with as many as five crore children and young people across the country and world with a view to inculcate positive qualities in them. He shares a close bond with them and has influence over them. Many people claim that their lives underwent a change after a meeting with this visionary. In the preceding pages, we have mentioned several values that he wishes to inculcate in people. We feel the following need a discussion afresh.

Entrepreneurship

Dr. Kalam finds entrepreneurship as an essential quality; he asserts that it should be a quality that should be inculcated in the educational process. He says:

"...Inquiry, creativity, technology, entrepreneurial and moral leadership are the five capacities required to be built through the educational process. If we develop in all our students these five capacities, we will produce 'autonomous learners': self-directed, self-controlled, lifelong learners who will have the capacity of both, to respect as well as question the authority in an appropriate manner."

If we look at our educational system, we find that as many as three million students graduate per annum from 300 universities, who set out to seek jobs, but there is no matching generation of employment where all of them can be assimilated. This results in augmenting the number of educated unemployed youths in almost all regions of the country. This gap is due to the mismatch between the skills required for the modern economy and the education imparted to our students. Moreover, investments and economic growth have not kept pace with the availability of human resources, and this gap has resulted into problems more than one in number.

Dr. Kalam lays utmost emphasis on cultivation of entrepreneurship skills that, in conjunction with other qualities, will help to bridge the gap. In his own words:

"...The educational system should highlight the importance of entrepreneurship and students during the college should be oriented towards setting up of the enterprises which will provide them creativity, freedom and ability to generate wealth. It should be taught to all the students that diversity of skills and perseverance in work makes (them) an entrepreneur."

He further stresses the need to include topics and practicals for entrepreneurship training in college syllabi for arts, science and commerce courses, so that education rises up to meet the demands of the modern society. He also expands the scope of those responsible for cultivating this quality when he says:

"The educational institutions, government and private enterprises should become facilitators for creating entrepreneurship schemes through the support of the banking system and the marketing system."

Spirituality

Spiritually, as is being given to understand in the present context, seems to be a contrived notion with an attempt to shape the young mind of the follower into it, little realizing that spirituality is something beyond it, and it can be found in different domains. Dr. Kalam deplores that in a majority of schools, particularly in the small towns, are, 'taming the young minds with dogma and obsolete concepts' rather than empowering them with freedom of inquiry. Commenting at this gloomy situation, he comments:

"Spirituality instead must form a vision of that which stands beyond, behind and within the passing flux of immediate things." He solemnly asks if it is inevitable to link spirituality to religion. He goes on to answer his own question thus:

"...It is important to know the distinction between spirituality in religion and spirituality as contrasting to religion. In the recent years, spirituality in religion has often carried connotations of a believer having faith more personal, less dogmatic, more open to new ideas and myriad influences, and more pluralistic than the faiths of established religions. It also can connote the nature of a believer's personal relationship or connection with his/her God or belief system, as opposed to the general relationship with the deity understood to be shared by all members of that faith."

Dr. Kalam takes spirituality as something real, 'to be explored by a close attention to our immediate world', though being waited upon to be realised. It is the, 'capacity to dream, visualising something which is a remote prospect', while remaining the greatest of present possibilities of life. He says that for him, spirituality is trust in the slow work of God. It is something that embeds us in harmonious relationships with others. He explicitly says:

"Spirituality is, indeed, all about connectivity with the cosmos. It can be described as a vision requiring the exercise of mind, heart and body."

Dr. Kalam was secular in spirit, he was none like the pseudo-secularists that we see around us in plenty. As he studied and visited different shades of spirituality, he realised that, 'there are many ideas and spiritual thoughts which transcend religions, geographies and time. If only we could bridge the spirituality among religions and nations, many of the problems like the gaps between the haves and the have-nots, deprivation causing unrest leading to extremism, the remnants of past animosities and war and several other roadblocks to peace and prosperity can be tackled'. He shares his experiences of peace, tranquillity and spirituality as he visited places of different faiths. He recalls these experiences thus:

Tawang Monastery, Arunachal Pradesh: Dr. Kalam recalls that he visited the Tawang Monastery in Arunachal Pradesh, located at an altitude of 3500 m, in the year 2003. As he stayed there for nearly a day, he noticed a unique condition not only in the monastery, but also in the adjoining villages where every face, young or old, radiated with happiness, despite the difficult wintry climate. In this 400-year-old monastery, he saw monks of all age groups in a state of serenity. He recalls this experience in his own words: "I asked myself, 'What is the unique feature of Tawang and surrounding villages which makes people and monks to be at peace with themselves?' When the time came, I asked the Chief Monk, 'How in Tawang villages and monastery, am I experiencing peace and happiness being radiated by everyone?' There was a pause, the Chief Monk smiled. He said, 'You are the President of India. You will know all about us and the whole nation.' Again, I said, 'It is very important for me, please give me your thoughtful analysis.'"

In the assembly of about 100 young and experienced monks, in the presence of a golden image of the Buddha, the Chief Monk and Dr. Kalam took their seats. The Chief Monk gave a short discourse, Dr. Kalam shares this discourse in these words:

"In the present world, we have a problem of distrust, unhappiness transforming into violence. This monastery spreads: when you remove 'I' and 'Me' from your mind, you will eliminate ego; if you get rid of ego, hatred towards fellow human beings will vanish; if hatred goes out of our mind, violence in thinking and action will disappear; if violence in our mind is taken away, peace springs in human minds. Then peace and peace and peace alone will blossom in the society."

Dr. Kalam advises that the youths will have to undertake the difficult mission to remove the ethos of 'I' and 'Me'. He solemnly advocates: "For this, we need the education inculcated in the young age as propagated by ancient philosophers."

Christian Monastery, Bulgaria: Dr. Kalam recalls the experience there as thus: "In my search for evolving a peaceful and prosperous society, I got a part answer. My search for the real truth continues. I visited an ancient Christian monastery in Bulgaria, where I had a discussion with the highly experienced monks on the message of Tawang. The Monk added that forgiveness is also the foundation of good life."

Birthplace of Swami Vivekananda: Dr. Kalam recalls his experience at the birthplace of Swami Vivekananda in these words: "Similarly, I had a memorable experience at the birthplace of Swami Vivekananda, a youth monk of India, who could keep the audience spellbound in eastern and western society with his inspirational messages of spirituality and practical life. I explained the Tawang experience to the disciples and they too felt the Tawang experience indeed as beautiful and added that the 'Trait of Giving' will add to peace and happiness."

Ajmer Sharif, Rajasthan: Dr. Kalam remembers his visit to this holy shrine and experience of spirituality in these words: "When I visited Ajmer Sharif, I participated in the Friday *Namaz*. Here, the Sufi expert told me that Almighty's creation, man, has been challenged with another powerful creation of Shaitan. Only good deeds lead to good thinking, good thinking results into actions radiating love as commanded by Almighty."

Big Thinking

For most people, it is true that they imagine the fanciful, but imagining is not thinking; you imagine something to forget, but you think when you intend to take some action, and this is the reason that 'big thinking', is a vital aspect of a successful life. The higher you aim, the higher your plane is where you work. If you aim at the ordinary, you can but attain ordinary accomplishments. Dr. Kalam mentions of the new opportunities available today, and exhorts the youth to think big and try to attain them. In his words:

"To take advantage of the boundless new opportunities and possibilities that are available today, you need two other things: faith and determination. Faith and determination are the two essential wheels needed to roll over the opportunities in life. Without them the real meaning of life can never be realised."

He explains that our faith, 'keeps us committed to pursuing our goals with all our vigour', while 'determination is the power that sees us through all our frustrations and obstacles'. When the power of determination is not hindered, one inevitably attains the desired goal, however high or sublime or transcendental it might be. Dr. Kalam says clearly:

"Decide that no matter what happens, you will do what you set out to do. If you are determined, despite all the distractions that you may face, you will be able to continue on your chosen path and remain focussed."

He also advises us to be realistic and says that it is not always easy to change the circumstances of life to suit your needs, but with your strength, faith and determination, you can successfully face them, and 'sometimes you may even be able to change the world itself'.

When asked if a person should keep aiming high, he solemnly advises: "Be optimistic and tenacious when facing adversities."

Conscience

When you set down to do a thing, you must be sure whether it is the right thing to do or not. Conscience plays a great role, and those who undermine it, cannot become exalted in mind and thinking. You must have seen many leaders, especially in the political field, who do not enjoy trust of the people despite a large following; and if you look at them closely, you will find that the followers are behind them only for the sake of vested interests. Dr. Kalam attaches a great importance to conscience. Let us quote his own words:

"Conscience is the divine light of the soul that burns within the chambers of our psychological heart. It raises its voice in protest whenever anything is thought of or done which is contrary to righteousness."

Immoral way of life begins to take root in our life the moment we try to suppress our conscience and fall for the transient favours, overlooking the lasting virtues. He describes it as, 'a form of truth that has been transferred through our genetic stock in the form of knowledge of our own acts and our feeling of right and wrong'.

Dr. Kalam delineates conscience as the judge that 'threatens, promises, rewards and punishes', though it remains an attribute that you can overlook, but only at the cost of your own degradation. Comparing conscience with the negative qualities that try to obstruct its path, he says that cowardice asks if it is safe, greed asks if there is any gain in it, vanity asks if he could become great, lust asks if there is pleasure in it, but conscience reigns supreme and asks a very simple question: "Is it right?"

It is very simple. Stick to conscience and you will find that the ultimate victory is yours. Ignore it, and you will not earn virtue despite all material possessions you happen to acquire.

Culture

Unity in diversity is a main feature of India, so to say, because as soon as we look inwards, we find several divisive forces at work, in the form of caste and religious politics. Dr. Kalam antagonises any attempt to divide people on religious lines, and wants all people to become united in a common bond, and this can be done when the commonalities of different religions can be brought out. Giving a formula to achieve this, he says:

"One aspect I realise is that the central theme of any religion is spiritual well-being. Indeed it should be understood that the foundation of secularism in India has to be derived from spirituality."

When we do not take pride in our common culture, we cannot rise to greatness. He further comments: "It is because our sense of mission has weakened our culture and ourselves. If we come to look upon ourselves as divided people with no pride in our past and no faith in the future, what else can we look forward to except frustration, disappointment and despair?"

He speaks very positively when people of one religion assume and adopt the other's features. He is very severe against fundamentalism and fundamentalist notions. He wants everybody to see the nation and religion in two distinct forms. Citing the example of A.R. Rahman, he says: "A.R. Rahman may be a Muslim but his voice echoes in the soul of all Indians, of whatever faith, when he sings *Vande Mataram*."

Dr. Kalam warns that the greatest danger to our sense of unity and our sense of purpose comes from those ideologists who seek to divide the people in the name of religion and, of course, other considerations. The Constitution of India bestows on all the citizens total equality under its protective umbrella. What is now the cause for concern is the trend towards putting religious form over relations and sentiments. He advises succinctly:

"The time has come for us to stop differentiating. What we need today is a vision for the nation which can bring unity. It is when we accept India in all its splendid glory that, with a shared past as a base, we can look forward to a shared future of peace and prosperity, of creation and abundance."

❒

17

Inspiring Stories from Life of Dr. Kalam

We have narrated a number of incidents, anecdotes and other events that occurred during the lifetime of Dr. Kalam. We suppose here are a few which the readers should know about. Just read on.

The Burnt *Roti*

Dr. Kalam remembers an anecdote from his childhood thus:

"When I was a kid, my Mom cooked food for us. One night, in particular when she had made dinner after a long hard day's work, Mom placed a plate of '*subzi*' and extremely burnt *roti* in front of my Dad. I was waiting to see if anyone noticed the burnt *roti*. But Dad just ate his *roti* and asked me how my day at school was. I don't remember what I told him that night, but I do remember that I heard Mom apologising to Dad for the burnt *roti*. And I'll never forget what he said: 'Honey, I love burnt *roti*.' Later that night, I went to kiss Daddy good night and I asked him if he really liked his *roti* burnt." He wrapped me in his arms and said: "Your Momma put in a long hard day at work today and she was really tired. And besides, a burnt *roti* never hurts anyone but harsh words do! You know, *Beta*, life is full of imperfect things... and imperfect people... I am not the best and am hardly good at anything! I forget birthdays and anniversaries just like everyone else. What I've learnt over the years is to accept each other's faults and choose to celebrate relationships."

Being Vegetarian

Despite the roaring controversy over meat-eating, there are a very large number of vegetarians in India, and Dr. Kalam was one of them. But he did not become a vegetarian out of choice, he was forced by his circumstances, but then he liked the food so much that he stuck on to it for all his life. Let us listen to the anecdote in his own words:

"My first dream was to get out of the isolation of Rameswaram island and its poor living conditions. My father understood my yearnings and encouraged me to move out and pursue my studies. There was no school beyond the primary level in Rameswaram, so at the age of twelve, I left home to study at Schwartz High School in Ramanathapuram. As I had very little money I had to learn how to survive on a tight budget. I opted for vegetarian meals at the school canteen instead of the non-vegetarian meals which I had been used to at home, since that meant a saving of three rupees every week. Three rupees a week seems a very paltry amount now, but in those days, it was a princely sum! I was ready for all kinds of hardships if it meant saving money and putting less burden on my family. Eating vegetarian food, I gradually started enjoying it, and till today, I continue to be a vegetarian."

Presence of Mind

As usual, it was a hot and humid day at Thumba. Kalam and his colleague, Sudhakar were working in the Payload Preparation Laboratory. As part of the pre-launch schedule, they were filling and remotely pressing the hazardous sodium and thermite mix. After the sixth such operation, Kalam and Sudhakar went into the payload room to confirm the proper filling of the mix. As they bent over to look into the tank, a drop of sweat from Sudhakar's forehead fell into the sodium, and before they could know what it was, there was a violent explosion which shook the entire room. It was so sudden that they did not know what to do for quite some time; but they had to regain their consciousness else their lives could have been at a great peril. The fire became fiercer with every passing moment, and water would not extinguish the sodium fire. Trapped in this inferno, Sudhakar, however, did not lose his presence of mind. He broke the glass window with his bare hands and literally threw Kalam out to safety before jumping out himself. Kalam touched Sudhakar's hands in gratitude, he was smiling through his pain. Sudhakar had to be hospitalised for a few days, but his presence of mind and gratitude were etched on Kalam's mind for all times to come.

Keeping Appointment

There were about 70 scientists working at a project of national importance under the supervision of Dr. Kalam; the work was hectic and long, and could take months; but all of them were motivated to do their best. Sometimes, they felt frustrated owing to the pressure of the work, but inspirational leadership of Dr. Kalam kept them on the right course. They not only worked hard, but also had to work late into the evening daily as they were required to complete the project in a given time frame. But there are occasions when the demands of wives and children have to be looked after too.

There was an exhibition in town and a little child wanted to go. He impressed upon his father, a scientist working under Dr. Kalam on this project, to leave office early and take him to the exhibition. The scientist gathered his courage and sought permission to go early that day. Dr. Kalam consented with the well-known perennial sleek smile that always graced his lips. But could the scientist go? No... he was so busy and engaged in his work that he forgot his appointment with his child. Finally, when he raised his head to look at the wall clock, he was stunned to see it showing half-past eight. He knew he was in trouble. He looked for his Boss, but he was not there. He had taken permission to go early, but he was already late. So, he hurriedly arranged his things and closed the cabin before walking away to his house with heavy steps. He knew he would have to deal with an unpleasant situation at home, and he was trying to brace himself for it.

Feeling guilty, he stepped into the drawing room where his wife sat. He meekly sat down and waited for his wife to say some harsh words. But he was unnerved when she calmly asked, "Would you like to have coffee or shall I straight away serve dinner if you are hungry?"

The man still felt nervous. He said softly, "If you would like to have coffee, I too would have it. But what about the child?"

There was surprise in store for him. She said, "Don't you know? Your Manager came and said that you were busy, and he took the child to the exhibition."

A sleek smile appeared on the man's face as he felt greatly relieved. He realised what had happened in fact.

At five o'clock, Dr. Kalam went to the scientist's cabin to remind him of his appointment with his child, but when he peeked into the cabin, he found him totally absorbed in his work. The way he worked, it was sure that he was going to miss the deadline. So, Dr. Kalam went to his house, took the child with him to the exhibition so that his promise could be kept without disturbing him from his work.

These are the qualities that make an ordinary person a legend in the eyes of his staff. Dr. Kalam displayed just one in this incident. If he demanded hard work from his staff, he also looked after their well-being to the highest extent. These are the qualities that inculcate spontaneous loyalty in the staff, and raise a leader towards greatest accomplishments.

We Shall Overcome

In 1979, a six-membered team was working on the flight version of a complex second stage control system for a static test and its evaluation. The team was in the countdown mode at T-15 minutes (that is, 15 minutes before the test). One of the twelve valves did not respond during the checkout. Anxiety drove the members to the test site to look into the problem. Suddenly, the oxidizer tank, filled with red fuming nitric acid (RFNA) burst causing severe burns to the team members. It was a very traumatic experience to see the suffering of the injured. Kalam, with the help of his colleague Kuru, rushed to the Trivandrum Medical College Hospital and begged to the wounded admitted.

Kalam kept vigil at the bedside of one Sivaramakrishnan all night, as he was grievously injured, yet he did not show signs of pain on his face, rather he kept expressing sincerity and optimism. In even acute pain, he mustered positive qualities. It is worth emulating. Kalam wrote about him thus, "Men like Sivaramakrishnan are a breed apart... This event greatly enhanced my confidence in my team; a team that would stand like a rock in success and failure."

Children are Foremost

Dr. Kalam was very fond of children, this was the reason that he delivered lectures to them by the scores. He always obliged whenever children wanted to meet him. He also gave children precious time and listened to them carefully to have the ideas the kids had. Once, after an address to a gathering of students and teachers, he invited students to ask questions. An overenthusiastic teacher sprang up and started to speak. At this, Dr. Kalam interrupted him, "Not now, first the kids, that is more important. We can talk after that if we have time."

On another occasion, a schoolgirl had made a papier mache model, and it was published in a newspaper. Kalam suggested that the girl had done a great job and she must be invited to Hyderabad. She was finally invited with honour due to a guest, and was shown the actual Prithvi and given lunch with the scientists. Dr. Kalam ensured that he met the girl himself. He enquired of her about her studies, school, hobbies and other relevant things.

Duty Comes First

In 1983, Dr. Kalam was to present to the Defence Minister a project. The Defence Minister suggested some modifications to the presentation. So, he worked all night, and he could finish the work by early morning. He was at his breakfast table when he remembered that his niece Zameela's wedding was to take place that very evening at Rameswaram, and he could not make it, even if he took a flight to Madras (now Chennai), as he could not have reached Rameswaram by train from there. There was no air link between Madras and Madurai even, which could have helped him. He shrugged his shoulders and concentrated his thoughts to his presentation that was to take place in a short while.

The presentation won kudos; the Defence Minister praised it and promised to clear the project. At this time, Dr. Arunachalam was the advisor to the Defence Minister. He supported Kalam in the entire task. When the meeting was over and the Defence Minister stood up to go, Dr. Arunachalam told him about the wedding of Kalam's niece at Rameswaram. It was a great gesture on his part. The Defence Minister reciprocated. This was how, when Kalam landed at Madras, an air force helicopter took him to Madurai, from where he took the train to reach Rameswaram in time for the wedding. The words of Dr. Arunachalam were ringing in his ears, "You have earned this for your hard work of the last six months."

Compassion for Birds

During his stint with the DRDO (Defence Research and Development Organisation), he was discussing how to secure the perimeter of an important building. A suggestion came, "Why not put broken glass pieces on the boundary wall?"

Dr. Kalam outrightly rejected the suggestion. He said, "No, if we do that, birds will not be able to perch on the wall."

Mimicry

Dr. Kalam, during his visit to Bihar, stayed at the government guest house in Patna. Next day, he was agitated to see the breakfast served to him, it was the typical English breakfast comprising toast and jam. He immediately sent for the cook, who said, "Sir, most of the *Sahibs* who come from Delhi are served this breakfast."

"I am not a *Sahib*, I am an Indian," said Dr. Kalam. "Serve me something an Indian can eat."

The cook enthusiastically cooked hot *bhaat* (salted rice pudding) in some time and Dr. Kalam ate it happily. Later that day, when he was taking a stroll in the courtyard, he spotted a giant tamarind tree. He remarked to his secretary, "Look, these funny guys have such a big tamarind tree, but did not put even one in my *bhaat*. Why are we Indians bent upon mimicking the eating habits of the foreigners?"

An Inspiring Keynote

A few days after Dr. Kalam was to be the President, he visited a modest school. His security was minimal. As he was addressing the speech, the power went off. At this, he did not mind to take the charge himself. He walked right in the middle of the crowd and asked the students to surround him. He then spoke to 400 students with his bare voice, and delivered, as always, an inspiring keynote.

Helicopter Crash

Dr. Kalam was, on 30 September, 2001, flying in a helicopter from Ranchi to Bokaro to attend a meeting and also address students in a school. Mr. Samresh Singh, science and technology minister of Jharkhand, was with him. Suddenly, the helicopter experienced some problem in the rotor; the pilots warned the passengers that they should be ready for the worst. Just moments before the helicopter was about to land at Bokaro, the engine failed, and with this, the helicopter plummeted to the ground from a height of around 100 metres. Miraculously, everybody survived. Dr. Kalam maintained his calm in this moment of adversity too, though he was injured. Rather, he praised the pilots for their expertise and said that they deserved bravery awards. He thanked the Divine. Anything could have happened if the engine had failed just a few seconds before. Immediately, he left for the school for his scheduled programme despite the bad experience, which could have proved perilous. So spirited Dr. Kalam was.

Unfit Chair

At the convocation of IIT Varanasi, Dr. Kalam was the Chief Guest. There were five chairs on the stage, the centre one being for Dr. Kalam, the other four designated for the top university officials. Noticing his chair being bigger in size than the others, Dr. Kalam refused to sit on it and offered the Vice Chancellor to sit on it instead. The VC couldn't, obviously. No doubt, another chair was made available immediately for the Honourable former President!

Humour

Dr. Kalam did not lack sense of humour. Prime Minister Vajpayee was a bachelor, so was Dr. Kalam. When Dr. Kalam went to file his nomination papers for election to the post of the President, Vajpayee pointed out the marital status. Dr. Kalam quipped without a loss of time, "I am not only a bachelor, but also a *Brahmachari* (celibate)." Everybody burst in a peal of laughter.

Dignified Presidential Guests

On his first visit to Kerala after Dr. Kalam became the President, he was entitled to invite anyone to the Raj Bhavan as the Presidential Guest. You will be surprised who all he invited to this solemn function. Two of the dignified guests were a roadside cobbler and a small hotel-owner. Dr. Kalam had spent a significant time as a scientist in Trivandrum and he knew the cobbler, and so was the owner of the small hotel where Dr. Kalam would often have his meals.

Kalam's Propriety

On the occasion of swearing-in ceremony as the President, Dr. Kalam had received some guests from Rameswaram, who stayed with him first at the DRDO guest house and then in the Rashtrapati Bhavan. His brother stayed with him in his room. Dr. Kalam hired a private bus to ferry his guests to various places and events; no official car was used for this purpose, and he paid for their food and stay. Our leaders have much to learn from this exalted personality.

The Missing Project

An engineering college had organised a state-level inter-college tech fest. Science projects were included in it, but a rule was formed to keep only working models there, which could be either innovated or copied from some place. In a nutshell, anything moving with explanation of theory behind it was eligible to be part of the expo. A large number of college groups participated. There were some pretty impressive projects over there. The college authorities invited Dr. Kalam as the Guest of Honour. A little before he came, it was inspected by eminent teachers. One group had put up their project in which ordinary toys were turned into signal-controlled systems. They had actually converted an ordinary cheap toy-bus to clap, using a very low investment. However, on the D day, their project didn't operate as expected. The inspection group asked them to vacate the place as they could not allow a failed project to be there. It created an awkward gap there, and there was no time to make it up.

Dr. Kalam walked in. He listened to and observed every project, giving suggestions and comments, appreciating and suggesting better ideas. He even discussed the source of idea, etc. The interaction with him was nothing less than an awesome one. He went round the hall for a good 2.5 hours, and noticed the gap. He pointed to the abrupt vacant place, recently vacated by the failed project group.

A senior professor told him that the place was held by a group whose project had failed somehow. He apologised for the same. At this, Dr. Kalam calmly asked if it was possible to show him the demo of the failed project. The team was there in the hall as volunteers, they were immediately summoned to set up and play, explain whatever they had. In 5-8 minutes, that vacant space didn't exist. They spoke about their demo. Dr. Kalam listened to them, and had a close look. He asked them what could be the possible cause of the device not working. The need of the team said, it should be because of some IC had gone crazy. Dr. Kalam asked them if they would be able to fix it. They responded in the affirmative and said that all that they would need were silver foil and a solder iron. These things were arranged. It took a whole 30 minutes to set up the project. The team's project worked. He appreciated and left with the calm he had come with.

You could imagine what the teachers and students did after this. They clapped their hands until they pained, they whistled till their throats pained. They were indeed touched by God that day!

Black Flags

During his visit to Manipur, Dr. Kalam was shown black flags and the Manipur People's Liberation Front observed a twelve-hour general strike. They were protesting against the law and order problem and robberies taking place on the highways. Dr. Kalam took this in his stride and said that they were trying to raise their voice against their problems; they had the right to do so. He also instructed the authorities to see what could be done about their problems.

VIP Treatment to Scientists

When some ISRO scientists were returning from Kourou, French Guiana, after overseeing the testing of INSAT-4B communications satellite, they did not expect what was to follow at the Charles de Gaulle Airport in Paris. After checking their passports, the airport officers continued to escort them. Confused, the scientists asked if there was any problem when the officer said they had orders to do so.

A senior officer then asked them to access the VIP Lounge of the Airline as their flight was scheduled after three hours. When the scientists told them that they had economy tickets, the officer informed that President Dr. A.P.J. Abdul Kalam had boarded a flight from the same terminal a few hours back, and had informed them that the scientists from the ISRO would be using their services as there was a satellite launch. He also requested them to take care of them.

In spite of his busy schedule, Dr. Kalam remembered that there was a launch scheduled and that many scientists would be travelling to and from India to ensure a successful mission.

Science Brings Real Bliss

Science should eliminate pain, it should make life easy and interesting. Development in one field of science should help the other field too, which requires integration of different scientific fields. Dr. Kalam recalls one such incident in which he helped the suffering people with nuclear science. Let us know what he says about this experience:

"The fact that we have now developed for Agni, a re-entry structure, for which we have developed this new material. A very light material called carbon-carbon."

"One day an orthopedic surgeon from the Nizam Institute of Medical Sciences visited my laboratory. He lifted the material and found it so light that he took me to his hospital and showed me his patients. There were these little girls and boys with heavy metallic calipers weighing over three kg each, dragging their feet around."

"He said to me: 'Please remove the pain of my patients.' In three weeks, we made the floor reaction Orthosis 300-gram calipers and took them to the orthopaedic centre. The children didn't believe their eyes. From dragging around a three-kg load on their legs, they could now move around! Their parents had tears in their eyes. That was indeed supreme bliss!"

Dream, Think and Act

Once a student asked Dr. Kalam how he could realise his aspiration of becoming a nuclear scientist; he wanted his advice. Kalam mildly smiled and said in an affectionate tone: "Dream, dream, dream. Think, think, think. And then put that into action, action, action. OK?"

He noted, "The biggest problem Indian youth faced, I felt, was a lack of vision, a lack of direction...What I wanted to say was that no one, however poor, underprivileged or small need feel disheartened in life."

Eating from His Plate

A student remembers this exhilarating experience: When some Indian students met him during the International Space Development Conference (ISDC) at San Diego, California, in 2013, they went up to his dining table to say 'hello'. The President, who was eating the dinner, asked a student to eat from his plate. Highly surprised, he took a leaf of spinach from his salad when he insisted. "Till this day, I take it to be a leaf of inspiration from him and the best dinner I could ever imagine," he shared.

Backbencher Wins an Internship

The students of a particular batch at the IIM Indore, were to give a presentation to Dr. Kalam in groups. Since this was a big chance to impress the President, everyone was trying hard, except this one group of so-called casual students, the backbenchers. They started working just two days before the D day. One of the students took the responsibility to format the presentation. While the content took half a day, he took one and a half days with no sleep to add colour, formatting and animation to the slides.

When the group presented the presentation, Dr. Kalam asked who did the formatting. He gave that guy a golden visiting card saying "ex-President India", printed on it and asked him to call at the office after two days. When the guy made the call, he was told that he had been chosen for an internship at his office and would be working on various presentations that he needed for the UNO.

Grinder's Payment

The Sowbhagya Enterprises, Erode (Tamil Nadu), a manufacturer of wet grinders, gifted Kalam with a grinder. Now, though he wanted one for his house, he refused to accept it as a gift. So, he wrote out a cheque of Rs 4,850 in favour of Sowbhagya Enterprises Pvt. Ltd.

The people at the Sowbhagya were very honoured by the gesture and instead of encashing the cheque, they framed it and proudly exhibited it in their office.

Two months later, they received a call from Kalam's office demanding that the cheque be deposited soon, and if not, the grinder would be returned.

This single incident reveals many qualities of his mind and heart.

Dhabas as Places of Experiments

During his visits to Uttar Pradesh, Dr. Kalam often ensured that his motorcade stopped at *dhabas* (roadside eateries) so that he could get a cup of piping hot tea and conduct an unusual experiment on rural entrepreneurship.

The *dhabas* that he chose to stop at were ordinary ones, serving tea in plastic cups to the great man who sat in a plastic chair alongside others. So, what was it that drew the 'Missile Man' to the *dhabas* of Uttar Pradesh? Kalam calmly told the *Hindustan Times*, "It's not tea, but the tea-seller!"

Expanding on the issue, he explained, "The whole idea is to discover how one man, let's say the roadside tea-seller, serves tea to nearly 100 or more people in a day and, at the same time, cleans utensils, collects money and welcomes customers with a smile. It's this spirit of serving that is so fascinating, one which needs to be inculcated and celebrated."

That was at the time when Srijan Pal Singh, the Lucknow-born IIM-Ahmedabad alumnus, had decided to work with Kalam instead of with a multinational, thus starting a trend of IIM students sacrificing plum jobs to intern with the former President.

Singh, who was with Kalam during his visits to *dhabas*, said, "Those visits on the Moradabad-Rampur highway and Azamgarh were part of the plan to know how micro-entrepreneurs operate in India and what value addition can enhance their earning potential."

He added: "India needs millions of such micro-entrepreneurs at the grass roots level. And we need to find how technology, marketing and quality management can improve such ventures. It is, in many ways, linked to (Kalam's) goal of 'providing urban amenities in rural areas' or PURA as it is promoting self-sufficed job generators."

The idea, Singh said, emerged from discussions that Kalam had with his team about how the real flavour of India is in its roadside markets. Singh said such unscheduled stops at *dhabas* helped establish that the *'chaiwallah'* too has a management lesson to teach.

Alongside his visits to *dhabas*, Kalam also began meeting grass roots innovators and product designers to discover ways to empower India. This was a great way of learning and understanding grass roots enterprises, a necessary element for planning to empower millions of rural and suburban people, said members of Kalam's team.

His staff was instructed to ensure that during his visits to smaller cities and rural areas, some time was set aside for interacting with local innovators and researchers. The *dhaba* experience was part of this.

Nehru Collar

Two beige suits, tucked away on a shelf in Ashish Jain's shop at Karol Bagh, will never be worn by the very special customer they were stitched for: A.P.J. Abdul Kalam. The former President is, unfortunately, no more with us.

According to Jain, Kalam had refused to come to the Fairdeals, the shop which had tailored his suits for nearly two decades, after he became the President of India. He did not want the entourage of security personnel, which would inevitably accompany him, to inconvenience the locals in the area or disrupt their schedules, according to Jain.

He informs that Kalam visited the shop for the first time 20 years ago, and soon became a regular customer. "We mostly made *bandgalas* with open necklines, an attire which came to be popularly known as the Kalam style. Dr. Kalam felt that the collar of the suit, we had stitched for his oath-taking ceremony in 2002, was uncomfortably tight. So, he asked us to redesign the suit with an open collar. That's how the *bandgalas* with open necklines came about," Jain said.

When Jain and his tailors referred to the suits as Chinese collars, Kalam corrected them. "He told us, 'no Chinese collar. Be Indian, call it the Nehru collar'," he recalled.

❐

Bibliography

The Very Best of A.P.J. Abdul Kalam – The Righteous Life, Rupa Publications India, 2014.
Wings of Fire: An Autobiography, A.P.J. Abdul Kalam, University Press, 1999.
Forge Your Future, A.P.J. Abdul Kalam, Rajpal & Sons, 2014.
India 2020: A Vision for the New Millennium, A.P.J. Abdul Kalam and Y.S. Rajan, Penguin Books India, 1998.
A.P.J. Abdul Kalam: Scientist and Humanist, Atulindra Nath Chaturvedi, Rupa Publications India, 2002.
Songs of Life, A.P.J. Abdul Kalam, Ocean Books, 2015.
Ignited Minds, A.P.J. Abdul Kalam, Penguin Books India, 2002.
The Scientific Indian, A.P.J. Abdul Kalam and Y.S. Rajan, Penguin Books India, 2010.
A.P.J. Adul Kalam: A Life, Arun Tiwari, Harper Collins Publishers India, 2015.
Wisdom of Kalam, Prashant Gupta, Ocean Books, 2012.
You Are Born To Blossom: Take My Journey Beyond…, A.P.J. Abdul Kalam and Arun K. Tiwari, Ocean Paperbacks, 2015.
You Are Unique, A.P.J. Abdul Kalam, Punya Publishing, 2012.
Turning Points: A Journey Through Challenges, A.P.J. Abdul Kalam, Harper Collins Publishers India, 2012.
Spirit of India, A.P.J. Abdul Kalam, Rajpal & Sons, 2010.
A Manifesto for Change, A.P.J. Abdul Kalam and V. Ponraj, Harper Collins Publishers India, 2014.

My Journey: Transforming Dreams into Actions, Rupa Publications India, 2013.
Governance for Growth in India, A.P.J. Abdul Kalam, Rupa Publications India, 2014.
The Family and the Nation, Acharya Mahapragya and A.P.J. Abdul Kalam, Harper Collins Publishers India, 2008.
The Kalam Effect: My Years with the President, P.M. Nair, Harper Collins Publishers India, 2008.

□□□